W9-BGA-799

THE 17 INDISPUTABLE
LAWS OF TEAMWORK
WORKBOOK

Embrace Them
and Empower Your Team

JOHN C. MAXWELL

Publishers Since 1798

THOMAS NELSON PUBLISHERS®
Nashville

A Division of Thomas Nelson, Inc.
www.ThomasNelson.com

Copyright © 2003 by Maxwell Motivation, Inc., a Georgia Corporation

All rights reserved. No portion of this book may be reproduced, stored in a retrieval system, or transmitted in any form or by any means—electronic, mechanical, photocopy, recording, or other—except for brief quotations in printed reviews, without the prior permission of the publisher.

Published in Nashville, Tennessee, by Thomas Nelson, Inc.

ISBN 0-7852-6576-7

Printed in the United States of America

03 04 05 06 BVG 6 5 4 3 2 1

CONTENTS

INTRODUCTION

Every day, in some way, you are part of a team. The question is not, "Will you participate in something that involves others?" The question is, "Will your involvement with others be successful?" The answer to that question can be found in this workbook.

Everyone knows that teamwork is a good thing—in fact, it's essential! But how does it really work? What makes a winning team? Why do some teams go straight to the top, seeing their vision become reality, while others seem to go nowhere?

These are questions that don't have simple answers. If it were that easy, sports would have more back-to-back world champions, and the list of Fortune 500 companies wouldn't change year after year.

One of the challenges of learning about teamwork is that even people who've taken a team to the highest level in their field sometimes have a hard time putting their finger on what separates a great team from a collection of individuals who can't seem to get it together. Some will say that the key to winning is a strong work ethic. But haven't you known plenty of hardworking individuals who never worked together to reach their potential? Others believe that great teams are the result of chemistry. They say, "I can't explain how you create it, but I definitely know it when I see it." How can you get your hands around that and learn from it to build *your* team?

My desire is to make team building simple to grasp, retain, and put into practice. I want to take the mystery out of it. That's why I've worked hard to identify the Laws of Teamwork. The wonderful thing about a law is that you can depend on it. No matter who you are, what your background is, or what circumstances you face, you can take laws to the bank.

This workbook has been written with the goal of helping you to accomplish the task of practicing and applying the laws. In the following pages I will challenge you to take a harder look at each law and how it applies to your life and teamwork potential. By answering questions and participating in activities, you will begin to identify how these laws affect your success and the success of the people in various areas of your life, such as family, work, volunteer organizations, and social circles.

Each law includes stories that will help you observe the law in action, questions to evaluate your own level of leadership, discussion questions to see how a particular law affects your organization, and an action section where you can improve your teamwork skills.

While most workbooks are designed in a weekly format that builds throughout the study, this is not the case with *The 17 Indisputable Laws of Teamwork Workbook.* Each law can stand on its own. And as you read about the laws, you may recognize that you already practice some of the principles effectively, or you may discover an area of weakness that you didn't know you had. For example, you may already understand and apply the *Law of the Big Picture,* but you could benefit by taking a closer look at the *Law of the Scoreboard.* It's up to you where to start and how many laws to cover. This is your study. I encourage you to personalize it!

You can certainly learn the laws of teamwork on your own using this workbook. However, since teamwork is about working with people, this workbook has been set up so that groups can learn about the laws together. The first four sections of each chapter (Read, Observe, Learn, Evaluate) are to be completed individually, and the last two sections (Discuss, Take Action) are best reviewed in a group setting.

If you are leading a group through this workbook, you can find a leader's guide with additional suggestions and instructions for these two sections at www.LawsOfTeamwork.com/Workbook. Since members of the group will have different areas of strength and weakness, I suggest you work your way through the study covering each law. That way, members of the group can learn from each other while improving their teamwork skills.

Whether you are a follower who is just beginning to discover the impact of teamwork or a natural leader who has already formed a team, you can learn from this workbook. Each law is like a tool, ready to be picked up and used to help you achieve your dreams and add value to other people. Pick up even one, and you will become a better team member. Master them all, and you will see great improvements in yourself and your team.

So come on, let's open the toolbox and get started!

THE LAW OF SIGNIFICANCE

One Is Too Small a Number to Achieve Greatness

❦ READ ❧

When you look at the ways people conduct their lives, you can tell pretty quickly who recognizes and embraces the truth of the *Law of Significance*. This is certainly true of Lilly Tartikoff. I don't know whether Lilly always knew the value of teamwork, but I suspect she learned it early. Lilly was once a professional ballet dancer. If dancers don't work together, their performances never reach the caliber of Lilly's. Beginning at age seven, she spent ten hours a day, six days a week practicing or performing ballet. As a result, she became a member of the New York City Ballet Company from 1971 to 1980.

At a tennis party in Los Angeles in 1980, Lilly met Brandon Tartikoff, the newly named president of entertainment for NBC. At that time he was the youngest network president in history at age thirty. They soon became friends. Then they began to see each other romantically. They were married in 1982. And that started a whole new life for

Lilly. She went from a non-television watcher to the spouse of a network executive immersed in the culture of the L.A. entertainment industry. But that adjustment was nothing compared to the other challenge she faced that year. For the second time in his life, Brandon was diagnosed with Hodgkin's disease.

On the advice of a physician friend, Brandon went to see a young oncological researcher at UCLA named Dennis Slamon. In August 1982, Dr. Slamon started Brandon on two kinds of treatment, one of which was experimental. Brandon would usually receive treatment on a Friday, and afterward Lilly would drive him home and take care of him while he suffered from horrible side effects all weekend. They did this for a year, and all the while Brandon continued in his role as network president. It was a difficult time for them, but they chose to face the cancer as a team, and in time Brandon recovered.

Out of that ordeal came many things. For one, Brandon's network, NBC, went from worst to first in the ratings. In his autobiography he wrote, "Cancer helps you see things more clearly. The disease, I've found, can actually *help* you do your job, and there's a very simple reason why: There's nothing like cancer to keep you focused on what's important."[1] That focus enabled him to air some of the most popular and groundbreaking shows in television's history: *The Cosby Show, Cheers, Hill Street Blues, Miami Vice, The Golden Girls, The A-Team, St. Elsewhere,* and others.

For Lilly, though, there was a different kind of outcome. Once Hodgkin's disease had been driven from her husband's body, she didn't simply move on.

"Brandon was at the receiving end of some pretty amazing science," she observed. The medical research that had extended Brandon's life intrigued her. So when she had an opportunity to help others benefit from that same science, she couldn't say no. This occurred in 1989 when Dr. Slamon, the UCLA scientist who had treated Brandon seven years earlier, asked Lilly for her help.

For years he had been studying breast cancer, and he believed he was on the verge of developing a radical new treatment that would not only be more effective in treating the disease than anything previously developed, but he could do it without all the usual side effects of chemotherapy. He had the expertise and skill necessary to do the work, but he couldn't do it alone. He needed someone to help with funding. And he thought of Lilly. She was only too happy to help.

The plan she developed showed great insight into teamwork and strategic partnerships. Lilly had once worked as a beauty adviser for Max Factor, formerly connected to Revlon. She sought to get Ronald Perelman, the CEO of Revlon, together with Dr. Slamon. At first that wasn't easy, but once Perelman realized the potential of Slamon's research, he pledged $2.4 million to the scientist's work, with no restrictions. It was a partnership unlike anything that had been done before. What resulted was the creation of the Revlon/UCLA Women's Cancer Research Program—and a successful new treatment for cancer that was soon saving women's lives.

For Lilly, cofounding the research program was just a beginning. She had gotten a taste of what teamwork could do, and she was hungry to do much more. She quickly realized that she could enlist others to her cause. She would build a larger team, and she would use her show business connections to do it. That same year she established an annual Fire and Ice Ball in Hollywood to raise money. A few years later, she enlarged her circle and partnered with the Entertainment Industry Foundation (EIF) to put together the Revlon Run/Walk, first in Los Angeles and then in New York. So far, those events have raised more than $18 million for cancer research. And in 1996 she helped create the National Women's Cancer Research Alliance.

Sadly, in 1997 Brandon's cancer recurred a third time and took his life. He was only forty-eight years old. Despite the personal setback, Lilly continues to build teams to fight cancer. Recently when she met Katie Couric, who had lost her husband to colon cancer, Lilly was again inspired to action. With the help of Couric and the EIF, in 2000 she formed the National Colorectal Cancer Research Alliance.

"When I sat down with Katie," said Lilly, "to hear that, with an early diagnosis, you could turn the cancer around—and that literally it's 90 percent curable and preventable . . . Well, this was like putting a steak in front of a hungry dog . . . I thought, *We've got to do this.* So I brought in all my partners: the Entertainment Industry Foundation and Dr. Slamon . . . And Dr. Slamon brought together an agenda and a mission . . . So we created the NCCRA [National Colorectal Cancer Research Alliance]. You have no idea how exciting and gratifying it is."[2]

When you look at the incredible, significant task Lilly Tartikoff and her partners are trying to accomplish—taking on cancer—it's clear that it cannot be done by an individual. But that's true of anything worth doing. If it's significant, it takes a team. That's something Lilly realized, put into practice, and now lives by every day. One is too small a number to achieve greatness.

❧ OBSERVE ❧

As much as we admire solo achievement, the truth is that no lone individual has done anything of significant value. The belief that one person can do something great is a myth. Even the Lone Ranger wasn't really a loner. Everywhere he went, he rode with Tonto! For the person trying to do everything alone, the game really is over. If you want to do something big, you must do what Dr. Slamon and Lilly Tartikoff did and partner with others.

1. What teams had Lilly already been a part of prior to her partnership with Dr. Slamon?

    _____

    _____

    _____

    _____

2. Why did Dr. Slamon invite Lilly to become part of his team? What value did she bring to the team?

    _____

    _____

    _____

3. Why is Revlon a strategic partner for breast cancer research?

    _____

    _____

    _____

4. How would Dr. Slamon's progress be affected if his team did not have a corporate sponsor?

    _____

    _____

    _____

    _____

5. In your industry or area of service, what group or organization is the model for the *Law of Significance?* How are they setting an example for successful teamwork?

_____

_____

_____

✺ LEARN ✺

A Chinese proverb states that "behind an able man there are always other able men." The truth is that teamwork is at the heart of all great achievement. The question isn't whether teams have value. The question is whether we acknowledge that fact and become better team players. That's why I assert that one is too small a number to achieve greatness. You cannot do anything of *real* value alone.

I challenge you to think of *one* act of genuine significance in the history of humankind that was performed by a lone human being. No matter what you name, you will find that a team of people was involved. That is why President Lyndon Johnson said, "There are no problems we cannot solve together, and very few that we can solve by ourselves."

C. Gene Wilkes, in his book *Jesus on Leadership*, observed that the power of teams is not only evident in today's modern business world. It has a deep history, which is illustrated in Scripture. He explains that

- Teams involve more people, thus affording more resources, ideas, and energy than would an individual.

- Teams maximize a leader's potential and minimize her weaknesses. Strengths and weaknesses are more exposed in individuals.

- Teams provide multiple perspectives on how to meet a need or reach a goal, thus devising several alternatives for each situation. Individual insight is seldom as broad and deep as a group's when it takes on a problem.

- Teams share the credit for victories and the blame for losses. This fosters genuine humility and authentic community. Individuals take credit and blame alone. This fosters pride and sometimes a sense of failure.

- Teams keep leaders accountable for the goal. Individuals connected to no one can change the goal without accountability.

- Teams can simply do more than an individual.

If you want to reach your potential or strive for the seemingly impossible—such as communicating your message two thousand years after you are gone—you need to become a team player. It may be a cliché, but it is nonetheless true: Individuals play the game, but teams win championships.

Why Do We Stand Alone?

Knowing all that we do about the potential of teams, why do some people still want to do things by themselves? I believe there are a number of reasons:

1. Ego

Few people are fond of admitting that they can't do everything, yet that is a reality of life. There are no supermen or superwomen. So the question is not whether you can do everything yourself; it's how soon you're going to realize that you can't.

Philanthropist Andrew Carnegie remarked, "It marks a big step in your development when you come to realize that other people can help you do a better job than you could do alone." If you want to do something really big, then let go of your ego, and get ready to be part of a team.

2. Insecurity

In my work with leaders, I've found that one of the reasons many individuals fail to promote teamwork is that they feel threatened by other people. Sixteenth-century Florentine statesman Niccolò Machiavelli probably made similar observations, which prompted him to write, "The first method for estimating the intelligence of a ruler is to look at the men he has around him."

I believe that insecurity, rather than poor judgment or lack of intelligence, most often causes leaders to surround themselves with weak people. As I stated in *The 21 Irrefutable Laws of Leadership,* only secure leaders give power to others. That is the *Law of Empowerment.* On the other hand, insecure leaders usually fail to build teams. This is usually due to one of two reasons:

- They want to maintain control over everything for which they are responsible, or
- They fear being replaced by someone more capable.

In either case, leaders who fail to promote teamwork undermine their own potential and erode the best efforts of the people with whom they work. They would benefit from the advice of President Woodrow Wilson: "We should not only use all the brains we have, but all that we can borrow."

3. Naïveté

John Ghegan, president of U.S. Business Advisors, keeps a sign on his desk that says, "If I had it to do all over again, I'd get help." That remark accurately represents the feelings of the third type of people who fail to become team builders. They naively underestimate the difficulty of achieving big things. As a result, they try to go it alone. Some people who start out in this group turn out okay in the end. When they discover that their dreams are bigger than their capabilities, they realize they won't accomplish their goals solo and they adjust. They make team building their approach to achievement. But some others learn the truth too late, and as a result never accomplish their goals. And that's a shame.

4. Temperament

Finally, some people aren't very outgoing and simply don't think in terms of team building and team participation. As they face challenges, it never occurs to them to enlist others to achieve their goal.

As a people person, I find this hard to relate to. Whenever I face any kind of challenge, the very first thing I do is think about who I want on the team to help. I've been that way since I was a kid. I've always thought, *Why take the journey alone when you can invite others along?*

I understand that not everyone operates this way. But whether or not you are naturally inclined to be part of a team is really irrelevant. If you do everything alone and never partner with other people, you create huge barriers to your own potential. Author and psychologist Dr. Allan Fromme quipped, "People have been known to achieve more as a result of working with others than against them." What an understatement! It takes a team to do *anything* of lasting value. Besides, even the most introverted person in the world can learn to enjoy the benefits of being on a team. And that's true even if he or she isn't trying to accomplish something great.

❧ EVALUATE ❧

Rate your own teamwork abilities by placing the number 1, 2, or 3 next to each of the following statements:

1 = Never   2 = Sometimes   3 = Always

_____   1. I enjoy being on a team.

_____   2. I see the value that different individuals bring to the team.

_____   3. Once I have a large goal in mind, I start to consider the people I will need to partner with to see that goal realized.

_____   4. When I am faced with a challenge, I ask for the advice of others.

_____   5. I consider my family to be a team.

_____   6. I consider those with whom I work to be members of a team, and I treat them as allies.

_____   7. I am at my best when working with others.

_____   8. I am willing to share the credit or victory with others.

_____   9. I realize that there are things I cannot accomplish on my own.

_____   10. My dreams and goals require a team.

_____   **Total**

24 – 30   This is an area of strength. Continue growing, but also spend time helping others to develop in this area.

16 – 23   This area may not be hurting you, but it isn't helping you much either. To strengthen your teamwork ability, develop yourself in this area.

10 – 15   This is an area of weakness in your teamwork. Until you grow in this area, your team effectiveness will be negatively impacted.

ᓚᕋ DISCUSS ᒳᕦ

Answer the following questions and discuss your answers when you meet with your team.

1. Who are some of the people you admire? Beside each person's name list his or her accomplishments. Then list the people who were involved in helping them accomplish their goals.

     _____

     _____

     _____

     _____

     _____

     _____

2. Do you agree with the author that nothing of significant value has been achieved by a lone individual? Explain.

     _____

     _____

     _____

     _____

3. What do you consider to be the number one reason why people are hesitant about being on a team? How can this hesitation be dealt with or eliminated?

     _____

     _____

     _____

     _____

4. How has the *Law of Significance* been realized by the actions and accomplishments of your team?

_____

_____

_____

_____

_____

5. How have you benefited by being a member of this team?

_____

_____

_____

_____

_____

6. What challenges do you currently face that require teamwork?

_____

_____

_____

_____

_____

7. What challenge does another team member face that you could help with?

_____

_____

_____

_____

_____

TAKE ACTION

This week, when attempting an important activity that you would normally take on alone, recruit at least one person from your team to help with the project. Choose a person who is close to the same skill level as you, whom you will not have to teach a number of things in order to accomplish the project, or choose someone who will bring his or her own unique gifts and talents to the project. After completing the project, list the pros and cons of working with another person.

Pros	Cons
_____	_____
_____	_____
_____	_____
_____	_____
_____	_____
_____	_____
_____	_____
_____	_____
_____	_____
_____	_____

2

THE LAW OF
THE BIG PICTURE

The Goal Is More Important Than the Role

❧ READ ☙

President Abraham Lincoln once remarked, "Nearly all men can stand adversity, but if you want to test a man's character, give him power." Few people have more power than an American president. Being the so-called "leader of the free world" can certainly go to a person's head. But not Jimmy Carter. If you look at his career—from the time he was a school-board official, to his term in the White House and beyond—you can see that he was willing to take on nearly any role in order to achieve a goal he believed in. He has always embraced the importance of the big picture.

There is possibly no greater example of the *Law of the Big Picture* in Carter's life than his role in working with Habitat for Humanity. Habitat was officially founded by Millard and Linda Fuller in 1976, though the two had been exploring the idea for many years before that—first in the U.S. and then overseas. The goal of the organization is a huge one—to eliminate poverty housing and homelessness from the world.

In the late seventies and early eighties, they began their bold venture. After six years, they had built houses internationally in Mexico, Zaire, and Guatemala. In the U.S. they had affiliates building houses in San Antonio, Texas; Americus, Georgia; Johns Island, South Carolina; and other locations in Florida and Appalachia. And groundwork was being laid to build in many other cities.

But the process was a struggle. They had found a successful formula for their goal: Offer home ownership to the neediest people able to make a house payment, build low-cost housing using volunteer labor, involve the future homeowner in the building process, and create no-interest loans to finance the houses. It was a great idea, and it was catching on. But to reach the world as they desired, the Fullers knew they would have to take Habitat to a whole new level.

From their headquarters in the town of Americus in southern Georgia, the Fullers saw a possibility. Ten miles away in the tiny town of Plains was a man who might be able to help them: Jimmy Carter. The former U.S. president had spoken at a couple of Habitat functions. Following Carter's speaking in 1983, Millard Fuller got the idea to approach Carter about helping the project along. And in early 1984 they made contact. When Carter said he was very interested in Habitat for Humanity, Fuller decided to boldly propose a list of fifteen possible roles the former president could take, hoping he would agree to one or two. His list included service on Habitat's board, making media contacts, helping to raise money, participating in a thirty-minute video, and working on a building crew for a day.

To Fuller's surprise, Carter agreed not only to one or two items on the list—he agreed to do *everything* on it. Ironically, the task that most captured the attention of the public was Carter's willingness to serve on a building crew and swing a hammer to help construct a house. At first people thought Carter would just stop by for brief publicity photos. But the former president put together a work crew, traveled with them via Trailways bus to the Brooklyn, New York, building site, worked tenaciously every day for a week, and slept in a church basement along with everyone else. That was in 1984. Since then Carter has raised teams and served in a similar fashion every year. And his dedicated service has attracted people from every walk of life to serve in similar roles.[1]

Habitat for Humanity is the brainchild of the Fullers, and its success is the result of the efforts of hundreds of thousands of people from around the globe. But Jimmy Carter is the one who put it on the map. His selfless service has inspired people rich and poor, obscure and famous, powerful and ordinary to see the huge goal of helping people at the lowest level of society by providing them with a decent place to live. And he inspired them to get involved.

So far, Habitat has built more than 100,000 houses sheltering more than half a million people all over the world.[2] Why? Because they, like Carter, wanted to be part of something bigger than themselves. They understood that the goal was more important than the role. They embraced the *Law of the Big Picture.*

❦ OBSERVE ❧

Winning teams have players who put the good of the team ahead of themselves. They want to play in their areas of strength, but they're willing to do what it takes to take care of the team. They are willing to sacrifice their role for the greater goal.

1. What attracted Jimmy Carter to Habitat for Humanity?

    _____

    _____

    _____

    _____

2. How did Jimmy Carter help to move Habitat for Humanity to the next level?

    _____

    _____

    _____

    _____

3. Why do you think Jimmy Carter was willing to participate physically in building a house?

    _____

    _____

    _____

    _____

4. In your industry or area of service, who models the *Law of the Big Picture*? How does this individual reflect the idea that the goal is more important than the role?

    _____

    _____

    _____

    _____

    _____

❦ LEARN ❧

People who build successful teams never forget that every person on a team has a role to play, and every role plays its part in contributing to the bigger picture. Without that perspective, the team cannot accomplish its goal, whether the team's "game" is sports, business, family, ministry, or government.

Leaders at the highest level understand the *Law of the Big Picture.* They continually keep the vision of the big picture before themselves and their people.

It takes courage and resolve to recognize that the goal is more important than the role. It's no small thing for people to do what's best for the team. Often it means sacrificing professional satisfaction, individual statistics, or personal glory. But as NBA-star-turned-successful-businessman Earvin "Magic" Johnson says, "Everybody on a championship team doesn't get publicity, but everyone can say he's a champion."

So how does a group of people start to become a more unified team? How do individuals make the shift from independent people to team players who exemplify the *Law of the Big Picture?* It's not something that happens overnight. It takes time. Here is my take on how to get the process started:

1. LOOK UP at the Big Picture

Everything starts with vision. You have to have a goal. Without one, you cannot have a real team. Hall of Fame catcher Yogi Berra joked, "If you don't know where you're going, you'll end up somewhere else." An individual without a goal may end up anywhere. A group of individuals without a goal can go nowhere. On the other hand, if the vision for achieving the big picture is embraced by everyone in a group, then those people have the potential to become an effective team.

Leaders usually have the role of capturing and communicating vision. They must see it first and then help everyone else to see it. The people on a team will sacrifice and work together *only* if they can see what they're working toward.

If you are the leader of your team, your role is to do what only you can do: paint the big picture for your people. Without the vision, they will not find the desire to achieve the goal.

2. SIZE UP Their Situation

One of the values of seeing the big picture is that it helps you recognize how far you really are from achieving it. Now, for someone determined to do everything alone, seeing the gulf between what is and what could be is often intimidating. But for people who live to build teams, seeing the size of the task ahead doesn't worry them. They don't shrink from the challenge—they savor the opportunity. They can't wait to put together a team and a plan to accomplish that vision.

3. LINE UP Needed Resources

Hawley R. Everhart believes, "It's all right to aim high if you have plenty of ammunition." That's what resources are: ammunition to help you reach a goal. It doesn't matter what kind of team you're on. You cannot make progress without the support of the appropriate equipment, facilities, funds, and so forth—whether your goal is climbing a mountain, capturing a market, or creating a ministry. The better resourced the team is, the fewer distractions the players will have as they work to achieve their goal.

4. CALL UP the Right Players

When it comes to building a successful team, the players are every-thing. You can have great vision, a precise plan, plenty of resources, and excellent leadership, but if you don't have the right people, you're not going to get anywhere. You can lose with good players, but you cannot win with bad ones.

5. GIVE UP Personal Agendas

Teams that win have players who continually ask themselves, "What's best for the rest?" They continually set aside their personal agenda for the good of the team. Their motto can be expressed by the words of Ray Kroc, founder of McDonald's, who said, "No one of us is more important than the rest of us."

One of the great sports stories from several years ago was the success of the U.S. women's soccer team. They remarkably won the Olympic gold medal and the World Cup in a few years' time. One of the key players on that team was Mia Hamm. In her book *Go for the Goal*, she gives her perspective on her sport and the attitude a player must bring into the game to achieve the goal of becoming a champion:

> Soccer is not an individual sport. I don't score all the goals, and the ones I do score are usually the product of a team effort. I don't keep the ball out of the back of the net on the other end of the field. I don't plan our game tactics. I don't wash our training gear (okay, sometimes I do), and I don't make our airline reservations. I am a member of a team, and I rely on the team. I defer to it and sacrifice for it, because the team, not the individual, is the ultimate champion.

Mia Hamm understands the *Law of the Big Picture*. And by doing whatever it took to help her team—including washing the equipment—she demonstrated that the goal was more important than the role.

6. STEP UP to a Higher Level

Only when players come together and give up their own agendas can the team move up to a higher level. This is the kind of sacrifice required for teamwork. Unfortunately, some people would rather cling to agendas and pursue the path of their own inflated egos instead of letting go in order to achieve something greater than themselves.

As philosopher Friedrich Nietzsche said: "Many are stubborn in pursuit of the path they have chosen, few in pursuit of the goal." And that's a shame, because people who think only of themselves are missing the big picture. As a result, their own potential goes untapped, and the people who are depending on them are bound to be let down.

❦ EVALUATE ❦

Rate your own teamwork abilities by placing the number 1, 2, or 3 next to each of the following statements:

1 = Never   2 = Sometimes   3 = Always

_____   1. I understand the goal of my team.

_____   2. I am willing to give up my personal rights for the greater good of the team.

_____   3. I know each person's role on my team and how each person contributes to the team's goal.

_____   4. I am realistic when sizing up how far my team is from reaching a goal.

_____   5. I am not afraid of a challenge because I know I have the support of a team.

_____   6. I know the equipment and resources needed to accomplish a task.

_____   7. I feel that each person on my team is important, and I express this through my interaction with my teammates and others.

_____   8. I know my purpose for being on the team.

_____   9. I am willing to take a subordinate role for the good of the team.

_____   10. I constantly ask myself, "What is best for the team?"

_____   **Total**

24 – 30   This is an area of strength. Continue growing, but also spend time helping others to develop in this area.

16 – 23   This area may not be hurting you, but it isn't helping you much either. To strengthen your teamwork ability, develop yourself in this area.

10 – 15   This is an area of weakness in your teamwork. Until you grow in this area, your team effectiveness will be negatively impacted.

❦ DISCUSS ❧

Answer the following questions and discuss your answers when you meet with your team.

1. What are the six things a team member must do to promote unity within his or her team?

    _____

    _____

    _____

    _____

    _____

    _____

2. Which part of the Big Picture process (Look Up, Size Up, etc.) comes most naturally to you? Give an example.

    _____

    _____

    _____

    _____

3. Which part of the Big Picture process is the most difficult for you? How can you overcome this challenge to promote team unity?

    _____

    _____

    _____

    _____

4. How do the leaders of your team ensure that each person on the team knows what the Big Picture is? If the Big Picture isn't effectively expressed to the team, how can communication between the leaders and team members be improved?

_____

_____

_____

_____

5. How do the members of your team react when they are asked to give up their personal agendas? How do you react?

_____

_____

_____

_____

6. How does the _Law of the Big Picture_ apply to a project that your team is currently working on?

_____

_____

_____

_____

7. What can you do to ensure that you or others are not hindering the accomplishment of the Big Picture goal?

_____

_____

_____

_____

TAKE ACTION

This week, in some area of your life, take on a subordinate role in order to help a team reach a major goal. Once the goal has been met, answer the following questions.

1. What was your role in helping the team to succeed?
   _____
   _____

2. What challenges did you face?
   _____
   _____

3. Did you at any time try to take over the project? Explain.
   _____
   _____

4. How did the other team members react to you? Why?
   _____
   _____

5. What did you learn from this experience?
   _____
   _____

6. How did you feel when the team succeeded (or failed)?
   _____
   _____

7. What will you do differently next time?
   _____
   _____

THE LAW OF THE NICHE

All Players Have a Place Where They Add the Most Value

On January 20, 2001, the United States experienced a historic first: An African-American assumed the post of secretary of state, the highest cabinet post in the United States government. The man who took that position was Colin Powell. Columnist Carl Rowan remarked of the appointment, "To understand the significance of Powell's elevation to this extremely difficult and demanding post, you must realize that only a generation ago it was an unwritten rule that in the foreign affairs field, blacks could serve only as ambassador to Liberia and minister to the Canary Islands."

Powell's appointment was remarkable, but not just because it was groundbreaking. It was significant because, to put it simply, Colin Powell was the best individual in all of the United States to take on the role of secretary of state. George W. Bush, the president who appointed him, stated, "In this cause, I know of no better person to be the face and voice of American diplomacy than Colin Powell." He went on to note Powell's "directness of speech, his towering integrity, his deep respect for our democracy, and his soldier's sense of duty."[1] Bush recognized that each player has a place where he adds the most value. Powell's is running the State Department.

A soldier's sense of duty has been a vital part of the character of Colin Powell since his early twenties. At first, Powell entered college uncertain of what he wanted to do with his life. But it didn't take him long to find his identity in an ROTC unit called the Pershing Rifles at the City College of New York. It was there that he discovered real team-work for the first time in his life. In *My American Journey*, Powell wrote:

> My experience in high school, on basketball and track teams, and briefly in Boy Scouting had never produced a sense of belonging or many permanent friendships. The Pershing Rifles did. For the first time in my life I was a member of a brotherhood . . . The discipline, the structure, the camaraderie, the sense of belonging were what I craved. I became a leader almost immediately. I found a selflessness among the ranks that reminded me of the caring atmosphere within my family. Race, color, background, income meant nothing. The PRs [Pershing Rifles] would go the limit for each other and for the group. If this was what soldiering was all about, then maybe I wanted to be a soldier.[2]

As he approached graduation from college, there was no doubt in his mind. He gladly chose military life.

In the army, Powell seemed to achieve success everywhere he went, and quickly rose in rank. His love was commanding troops, and when he received those assignments he did well. He was constantly tapped for special jobs and responsibilities. When that happened over and over, keeping him from leading soldiers in the field, he became frustrated. But a mentor, General John Wickham, wisely told him, "You're not going to have a conventional army career. Some officers are just not destined for it."

Wickham was right. Powell's career did turn out to be unusual. And it ultimately prepared him for a cabinet post, sharpening his gifts and giving him broad experience. As an infantry officer who did tours around the globe (including two in Vietnam), Powell learned command and leadership. His work with soldiers also taught him to communicate and connect with people. As a White House Fellow, he got his first exposure to American politics and world governments. Besides his interaction with high-level U.S. officials, he met with leaders of Japan, the Soviet Union, China, Poland, Bulgaria, and West Germany.

Powell moved to a whole new level when he began working in the Pentagon during the Carter and Reagan administrations. It was there that he learned how to work with civil servants and to understand the workings of government and military politics. As the senior military assistant to Secretary of Defense Caspar Weinberger, Powell traveled the world and came to understand the complexity of interaction between the United States and foreign powers.

But it was in the office of the national security adviser that Powell stepped into the "big leagues." As the deputy assistant to the president for national security affairs, he gained valuable experience in foreign policy. In fact, he was so adept that when his boss, Frank Carlucci, was asked to be secretary of defense, Powell stepped into Carlucci's former position as national security adviser. There he not only advised President Reagan, but he also worked side by side with Secretary of State George Shultz as the statesman negotiated nuclear missile treaties with the USSR, organized summits between heads of state, and worked with Soviet President Mikhail Gorbachev to end the Cold War.

How does someone like Colin Powell top off a successful term as the nation's first African-American national security adviser? By achieving the military's highest rank of four stars, and then by becoming the youngest chairman of the Joint Chiefs of Staff in the history of the nation. (He was also that position's first African-American and first ROTC graduate.) And once again, Powell shone in his position. Les Aspin, former secretary of defense, commented about Powell following a meeting in the Clinton White House, "It was clear to all of us that he could do any job in the room, up to and including president."[3]

When President-elect Bush approached him about becoming a cabinet member, there was only one logical place for him to serve, the place where he would add the most. At a town hall meeting on January 25, 2001, Powell remarked:

> I didn't know I would be coming back into government when I left the Army seven years ago and went into private life . . . But when Governor Bush asked me to consider it, I was ready for it. I was anxious to see if I could serve again. I think I have something to contribute still. And when he specifically said, I would like you to go to the State Department, it was almost as if I had been preparing for this in one way or another for many, many years. My work in the Pentagon, my work as a deputy national security advisor, national security advisor, chairman of the Joint Chiefs of Staff, and seven years in private life watching the world change, suggested to me this is something I should do.[4]

President Bush, his cabinet, and everyone in the country have a lot to gain from Powell. Not only is he the best person for the job, but he has given the president and his team greater credibility with a constituency inclined not to trust them. Powell's appointment is tangible proof of

Bush's claim to inclusiveness. But that's the power of the *Law of the Niche*. When the right team member is in the right place, everyone benefits.

✑ OBSERVE ✑

Good things happen to a team when a player takes the place where he or she adds the most value. Great things happen when all the players on the team take the role that maximizes their strengths—their talent, skills, and experience.

1. What experiences prepared Colin Powell for the position of secretary of state?

   _____

   _____

   _____

   _____

   _____

2. Do you agree that the position of secretary of state was where Colin Powell would add the most value on President George W. Bush's team? Explain.

   _____

   _____

   _____

   _____

   _____

3. How did individuals and groups benefit from Colin Powell's appointment?

_____

_____

_____

_____

_____

4. Why was it important for Colin Powell to see the value he could bring to the position?

_____

_____

_____

_____

5. In your industry or area of service, what group or organization best models the *Law of the Niche?* How do they reflect the idea that all players have a place where they add the most value?

_____

_____

_____

_____

_____

ᲫᏚ LEARN ᎨᎥ

Having the right people in the right places is essential to team building. Take a look at how a team's dynamic changes according to the placement of people:

The Wrong Person in the Wrong Place	=	Regression
The Wrong Person in the Right Place	=	Frustration
The Right Person in the Wrong Place	=	Confusion
The Right Person in the Right Place	=	Progression
The Right People in the Right Places	=	Multiplication

It doesn't matter what kind of team you're dealing with, the principles are the same. David Ogilvy was right when he said, "A well-run restaurant is like a winning baseball team. It makes the most of every crew member's talent and takes advantage of every split-second opportunity to speed up service."

NFL champion coach Vince Lombardi observed, "The achievements of an organization are the results of the combined effort of each individual." That is true, but creating a winning team doesn't come just from having the right individuals. Even if you have a great group of talented individuals, if each person is not doing what adds the most value to the team, you won't achieve your potential as a team. That's the art of leading a team. You've got to put people in their place—and I mean that in the most positive way!

To be able to put people in the places that utilize their talents and maximize the team's potential, you need three things. You must . . .

1. Know the Team

You cannot build a winning team or organization if you don't know its vision, purpose, culture, history, and so forth. If you don't know where the team is trying to go—and why it's trying to get there—you cannot bring the team to the height of its potential. You've got to start where the team actually is; only then can you take it somewhere.

2. Know the Situation

Even though the vision or purpose of an organization may be fairly constant, its situation changes constantly. Good team builders know where the team is and what the situation requires. For example, when a team is young and just getting started, the greatest priority is often to just get good people. But as a team matures and the level of talent increases, fine tuning becomes more important. It's at that time that a leader must spend more time matching the person to the position.

3. Know the Player

It sounds obvious, but you must know the person you are trying to position in the right niche. I mention this because leaders tend to want to make everyone else conform to their images, to approach their work using the same skills and problem-solving methods. But team building is not the same as working on an assembly line.

Mother Teresa, who worked with people her whole life, observed, "I can do what you can't do, and you can do what I can't do; together we can do great things." As you work to build a team, look at each person's experience, skills, temperament, attitude, passion, people skills, discipline, emotional strength, and potential. Only then will you be ready to help a team member find his or her proper place.

Right now you may not be in a position to place others on your team. In fact, you may be thinking to yourself, *How do I find my own niche?* If that's the case, then follow these guidelines:

- **Be Secure:** My friend Wayne Schmidt says, "No amount of personal competency compensates for personal insecurity." If you allow your insecurities to get the better of you, you'll be inflexible and reluctant to change. And to grow you must be willing to change.

- **Get to Know Yourself:** You won't be able to find your niche if you don't know your strengths and weaknesses. Spend time reflecting on and exploring your gifts. Ask others to give you feedback. Do what it takes to remove personal blind spots.

- **Trust Your Leader:** A good leader will help you start moving in the right direction. If you don't trust your leader, look to another mentor for help. Or get on another team.

- **Look at the Big Picture:** Your place on the team only makes sense in the context of the big picture. If your only motivation for finding your niche is personal gain, your poor motives may prevent you from discovering what you desire.

- **Rely on Your Experience:** When it comes down to it, the only way to know that you've discovered your niche is to try what seems right and learn from your failures and successes. When you discover what you were made for, your heart sings.

❧ EVALUATE ❧

Rate your own teamwork abilities by placing the number 1, 2, or 3 next to each of the following statements:

1 = Never   2 = Sometimes   3 = Always

_____   1. I have a clear understanding of my organization's vision and purpose.

_____   2. I can easily explain my organization's unique culture.

_____   3. When I succeed at something, I take time to reflect on what I did right so I can learn from my accomplishments.

_____   4. I am in the place where I will add the most value to my team.

_____   5. I aggressively pursue personal growth in order to grow in my profession or area of service.

_____   6. I'm accurate when determining my strengths and weaknesses, and the reactions of my peers and other leaders support my self-evaluation.

_____   7. I trust my current leader and his or her use of my skills on the team.

_____   8. I have a mentor from whom I receive guidance and feedback on a regular basis.

_____   9. My motivation for excelling in my profession or area of service goes beyond my personal gain.

_____   10. When I fail at something, I take time to reflect on and analyze my mistakes in order to learn from the experience.

_____   **Total**

24 – 30   This is an area of strength. Continue growing, but also spend time helping others to develop in this area.

16 – 23   This area may not be hurting you, but it isn't helping you much either. To strengthen your teamwork ability, develop yourself in this area.

10 – 15   This is an area of weakness in your teamwork. Until you grow in this area, your team effectiveness will be negatively impacted.

ᐳᓬ DISCUSS ᓬᐳ

Answer the following questions and discuss your answers when you meet with your team.

1. Why is it important for a person to find his or her niche?

   _____

   _____

   _____

   _____

2. What steps should a person take to find his or her niche?

   _____

   _____

   _____

   _____

3. What steps have you taken?

   _____

   _____

   _____

   _____

4. How does your current position utilize your strongest skills and qualities?

   _____

   _____

   _____

   _____

5. How does your group's leader utilize the *Law of the Niche* when handing out assignments?

_____

_____

_____

_____

6. How could your team better utilize the *Law of the Niche* when attempting your next project?

_____

_____

_____

_____

7. What can you do to ensure that you are in the right place?

_____

_____

_____

_____

TAKE ACTION

You and each person on your team have a unique set of gifts, talents, and training. This week, if you have not done so already, take a personality test such as DISC or Myers-Briggs. Then fill out the survey below to better define your niche. Look for opportunities to use your strengths and find out if your organization has any opportunities that will allow you to improve or learn specific skills.

1. What job or task do you enjoy doing most? Why?

   _____

   _____

   _____

2. What job or task brings the greatest return or results?

   _____

   _____

   _____

3. What are your hobbies and interests?

   _____

   _____

   _____

4. What is your formal training (degrees, certifications, classes taken)?

   _____

   _____

   _____

5. Outside of your obvious job skills, what other skills or training do you have?

   _____

   _____

   _____

6. In what area do you think you would best serve the team?

   _____

   _____

   _____

7. What are your career goals?

   _____

   _____

   _____

8. How do you benefit from being a member of this team?

   _____

   _____

   _____

9. How does the team benefit from having you as a member?

   _____

   _____

   _____

10. What opportunities are available to you to work in your niche?

    _____

    _____

    _____

11. What learning opportunities are available to you to improve your skills?

    _____

    _____

    _____

THE LAW OF
MOUNT EVEREST

As the Challenge Escalates, the Need for Teamwork Elevates

✤ READ ✤

In 1935, twenty-one-year-old Tenzing Norgay made his first trip to Mount Everest. He worked as a porter for a British team of mountaineers. A Sherpa born in the high altitudes of Nepal, Tenzing had been drawn to the mountain from the time that Westerners began visiting the area with the idea of climbing to the mountain's peak. The first group had come in 1920. Fifteen years later, climbers were still trying to figure out how to conquer the mountain.

The farthest this expedition would go was up to the north col, an altitude of 22,000 feet. (A *col* is a flat area along a mountain's ridge between peaks.) And it was just below that col that the climbing party made a gruesome discovery. They came across a wind-shredded tent. In that tent was a skeleton with frozen skin stretched over the bones. It was sitting in an odd position, with one boot off and the laces of the remaining boot between its bony fingers.

Mountain climbing is not for the faint of heart. The world's highest peaks are some of the most inhospitable places on earth. Of course, that hasn't stopped people from attempting to conquer mountains. In 1786 the first climbers made it to the summit of Europe's highest mountain, Mont Blanc in France. That was quite a feat. But there's a big difference between climbing the highest of the Alps at 15,771 feet and climbing Everest, the world's highest peak, at 29,035 feet—especially in the days before high-tech equipment. Everest is remote. The altitude incapacitates all but the hardiest and most experienced climbers, and the weather is unforgiving. Experts believe that the bodies of 120 failed climbers remain on the mountain today.[1]

The body Tenzing and the others found in 1935 was that of Maurice Wilson, an Englishman who had sneaked into Tibet and tried to climb the mountain secretly, without the permission of the Tibetan government. Because he was trying to make the ascent quietly, he had hired only three porters to climb the mountain with him. As they approached the north col, those men had refused to go any farther with him. Wilson decided to try to make the climb on his own. That decision killed him.

Only someone who has climbed a great mountain knows what it takes to make it to the top. For thirty-two years, between 1920 and 1952, seven major expeditions tried—and failed—to make it to the top of Everest. Tenzing Norgay was on six of those expeditions, as well as many other high mountain climbs. His fellow climbers joked that he had a third lung because of his ability to climb tirelessly while carrying heavy loads. He earned their respect, and he learned a lot. The greatest lesson was that no one should underestimate the difficulty of the climb. He had seen people do that at a great price.

In 1953 Tenzing embarked on his seventh expedition to Everest with a British group led by Colonel John Hunt. By then he was respected not only as a porter who could carry heavy loads at high altitudes, but also as a mountaineer and full-fledged expedition member, an honor unusual for a Sherpa. The year before, he had climbed to a height of 28,250 feet with a Swiss team. Up to then, that was the closest any human being had come to the top of the mountain.

Tenzing was also engaged to be the British group's sirdar for the trip, the Sherpa leader who would hire, organize, and lead the porters for the journey. That was no small task. To get just two people from base camp up to the summit, the team brought ten high-altitude climbers, including a New Zealander named Edmund Hillary. Altogether, the men would require two and a half *tons* of equipment and food. Those supplies couldn't be trucked or airlifted to the base of the mountain. They would have to be delivered to Kathmandu and *carried* on the backs of men and women 180 miles—up and down Himalayan ridges and over rivers crossed by narrow rope-and-plank bridges to the base camp. Tenzing would have to hire between two and three hundred people just to get the supplies in the vicinity of the mountain.

Supplies that would be needed by the party above the base camp would have to be carried up the mountain by another forty porters, each a Sherpa with extensive mountain experience. The best third of that team would continue working higher up the mountain, carrying the 750 pounds of necessary equipment in 30-pound loads. Only Tenzing and three other porters would have the strength and skill to go to the high camps near the summit.

For each level that the climbers reached, a higher degree of team-work was required. One set of men would exhaust themselves just to get equipment up the mountain for the next group. Two-man teams would work their way up the mountain by finding a path, cutting steps, and securing ropes. They would then be done, having spent themselves to make the next leg of the climb possible for another team. Of the team-work involved, Tenzing remarked, "You do not climb a mountain like Everest by trying to race ahead on your own, or by competing with your comrades. You do it slowly and carefully, by unselfish teamwork. Certainly I wanted to reach the top myself; it was the thing I had dreamed of all my life. But if the lot fell to someone else I would take it like a man, and not a cry-baby. For that is the mountain way."[2]

The team of climbers, using the "mountain way," ultimately made it possible for two pairs to make an attempt at reaching the summit. The first pair consisted of Tom Bourdillon and Charles Evans. When they tried and failed, the other team got its chance. That team consisted of Tenzing and Edmund. Tenzing wrote of the first team:

> They were worn-out, sick with exhaustion, and, of course, terribly disap-pointed that they had not reached the summit themselves. But still . . . they did everything they could to advise and help us. And I thought, Yes, that is how it is on a mountain. That is how a mountain makes men great. For where would Hillary and I have been without the others? Without the climbers who had made the route and the Sherpas who had carried the loads? Without Bourdillon and Evans, Hunt and Da Namgyal, who had cleared the way ahead? Without Lowe and Gregory, Ang Hyima, Ang Tempra, and Penba, who were there only to help us? It was only because of the work and sacrifice of all of them that we were now to have our chance at the top.[3]

They made the most of their chance. On May 29, 1953, Tenzing Norgay and Edmund Hillary accomplished what no other human being had ever done: They stood on the summit of Mount Everest, the world's highest peak!

❧ OBSERVE ❧

If you don't already do it, teach yourself to rally with your teammates. You cannot win a great challenge alone. As Tenzing asserted, "On a great mountain, you do not leave your companions and go to the top alone."[4]

1. What happened to the man who tried to climb Mount Everest alone?

    _____

    _____

2. What is the "mountain way"?

    _____

    _____

3. How did Tom Bourdillon and Charles Evans show their commitment to the team?

    _____

    _____

    _____

4. In your industry or area of service, what group or organization is the model for the _Law of Mount Everest?_ How does this group reflect the idea that as the challenge escalates, the need for teamwork elevates?

    _____

    _____

    _____

    _____

❧ LEARN ☙

You may not be a mountain climber, and you may not have any desire to reach the summit of Everest. But I bet you have a dream. I say this with confidence because, deep down, everybody has one—even the people who haven't figured out what theirs is yet. If you have a dream, you need a team to accomplish it.

How do you approach the task of putting together a team to accomplish your dream? I think the best way to start is to ask yourself three questions:

1. What Is My Dream?

It all starts with this question, because your answer *reveals what could be.* What lies in your heart? What do you see as a possibility for your life? What would you like to accomplish during your time on this earth? Only a dream will tell you such things.

2. Who Is on My Team?

This second question tells you *what is.* It measures your current situation. Your potential is only as good as your current team. That's why you must examine who is joining you on your journey. A great dream with a bad team is nothing more than a nightmare.

3. What Should My Dream Team Look Like?

The truth is that your team must be the size of your dream. If it's not, then you won't achieve it. You simply cannot achieve a #10 dream with a #4 team. It just doesn't happen. If you want to climb Mount Everest, you need a Mount Everest–sized team. There's no other way to do it. It's better to have a great team with a weak dream than a great dream with a weak team.

One of the mistakes I've seen people make repeatedly is that they focus too much attention on their dreams and too little on their teams. The truth is that if you build the right team, the dream will almost take care of itself.

Every dream brings challenges of its own. The kind of challenge determines the kind of team you need to build. Take a look at a few examples:

Type of Challenge	Type of Team Required
New Challenge	Creative Team
Controversial Challenge	United Team
Changing Challenge	Fast and Flexible Team
Unpleasant Challenge	Motivated Team
Diversified Challenge	Complementary Team
Long-Term Challenge	Determined Team
Everest-Sized Challenge	Experienced Team

If you want to achieve your dream—I mean really do it, not just imagine what it would be like—then grow your team. But as you do so, make sure your motives are right. Some people gather a team just to benefit themselves. Others do it because they enjoy the team experience and want to create a sense of community. Still others do it because they want to build an organization. The funny thing about those reasons is that if you're motivated by *all* of them, then your desire to build a team probably comes from wanting to add value to everyone on the team. But if your desire to build the team comes as the result of only one of those reasons, you probably need to examine your motives.

When the team you have doesn't match up to the team of your dreams, then you have only two choices: *Give up* your dream or *grow up* your team. Here is my recommendation concerning how to do the latter:

1. Develop Team Members

The first step to take with a team that's not realizing its potential is to help individual team members to grow. If you're leading the team, then one of your most important responsibilities is to see the potential that people don't see in themselves and draw it out. When you accomplish this, you're doing your job as a leader!

Think about the people on your team and determine what they need, based on the following four categories:

- Enthusiastic Beginner—Needs Direction

- Disillusioned Learner—Needs Coaching

- Cautious Completer—Needs Support

- Self-Reliant Achiever—Needs Responsibility

Always give the people who are already on your team a chance to grow and bloom.

2. Add Key Team Members

Even if you give every person on your team a chance to learn and grow, and they make the most of those opportunities, you may find that you still lack the talent you need to accomplish your dream. That's when it's time to recruit new talent. Sometimes all the team needs is one key person with talent in an area to make the difference between success and failure.

3. Change the Leadership

Every challenge needs a leader with gifts and talents to lead the team as it meets that challenge. Some people believe that one person remains the team leader at all times. But that idea is false. It's what I call the "Myth of the Head Table." The same person cannot—and should not—always lead the team in every situation. As a team member, if you set that expectation for one leader, the team will never reach its potential. As a leader, if you put that expectation on yourself, you are destined for failure.

The challenge of the moment often determines the leader for that challenge. Why? Because every person on the team has strengths and weaknesses that come into play.

Everyone on the team has value. However, it's important to avoid another leadership misconception: the *Myth of the Roundtable*. It's the belief that everyone on the team is equal, that all opinions count the same, and that a team can function equally with anyone in charge. That isn't true either. When it came time for the Everest expedition to send someone to the top, only four men were determined to be up to the challenge. Colonel Hunt made the determination concerning who would make the climb. And because the right people were selected—based on ability—the whole team won.

If your team is facing a big challenge, and it doesn't seem to be making any progress "up the mountain," then it might be time to change leaders. There may be someone on the team more capable for leading during this season.

4. Remove Ineffective Members

Sometimes a team member can turn a winning team into a losing one, either through lack of skill or a poor attitude. In those cases you must put the team first and make changes for the greater good.

Growing a team isn't easy. It is demanding and time-consuming. But if you want to achieve your dream, you have no other choice. The greater the dream, the greater the team. And as the challenge escalates, the need for teamwork elevates.

EVALUATE

Rate your own teamwork abilities by placing the number 1, 2, or 3 next to each of the following statements:

1 = Never   2 = Sometimes   3 = Always

_____   1. When I set out to accomplish something great, one of my first thoughts is to build a team so that my dream will be realized.

_____   2. I evaluate the members of my team so I know what challenges we will be able to take on.

_____   3. I am equipped for the tasks my team works on.

_____   4. I focus just as much time on investing in my team as I do on reaching my goal.

_____   5. I would understand if a member of our team were removed for performance-based or character-based reasons.

_____   6. I would not consider the team successful if we didn't achieve the goal together.

_____   7. I am willing to invest my time in developing other people in order to realize my dream or the team's dream.

_____   8. I have a desire to help the members of my team realize their potential, and I spend time encouraging the members of my team in their areas of strength.

_____   9. I am open to new members being added to our team if the result will be greater success.

_____   10. I would be willing to take on a leadership role if it would best serve the team.

_____   **Total**

24 – 30   This is an area of strength. Continue growing, but also spend time helping others to develop in this area.

16 – 23   This area may not be hurting you, but it isn't helping you much either. To strengthen your teamwork ability, develop yourself in this area.

10 – 15   This is an area of weakness in your teamwork. Until you grow in this area, your team effectiveness will be negatively impacted.

❧ DISCUSS ❧

Answer the following questions and discuss your answers when you meet with your team.

1. How do you react to a huge challenge?

_____

_____

_____

2. How does your team gear up for a huge challenge?

_____

_____

_____

3. What changes have been made to your team in the last year? Why were these changes made?

_____

_____

_____

4. If you were to put together a "dream team" for the current project your team is working on, what would that team look like?

_____

_____

_____

_____

_____

5. What changes need to be made to your team in order to prepare for larger challenges?

   _____

   _____

   _____

6. What changes do you personally need to make to prepare for larger team challenges?

   _____

   _____

   _____

TAKE ACTION

The challenges that our teams face are not always ones we select. Sometimes they are thrust upon us, and we have no choice but to do the best we can with the team we have, or give up and suffer the consequences.

Based on your Big Picture goals, take some time to brainstorm possible situations that your team may face. Then brainstorm steps you can take to strengthen yourself and your team so you will be prepared to handle such situations. Start building today, so that when a formidable challenge occurs, you and your team will be ready.

Possible Challenges My Team Might Face

1. _____
2. _____
3. _____
4. _____
5. _____

Steps for Personal Growth

1. _____
2. _____
3. _____
4. _____
5. _____

Steps for Team Growth

1. _____
2. _____
3. _____
4. _____
5. _____

THE LAW OF THE CHAIN

The Strength of the Team Is Impacted by Its Weakest Link

On March 24, 1989, the news broke that an environmental disaster had occurred in Alaska's Prince William Sound. The oil tanker *Exxon Valdez* had run aground on the Bligh Reef, damaging the hull of the ship and rupturing eight of the vessel's eleven cargo tanks. As a result, 10.8 million of the ship's approximately 53 million gallons of oil spilled out of the ship and into the sea.

The negative impact on the area was immense. Fishing and tourism came to a halt, harming the local economy. The environment suffered greatly. And though it wasn't the largest oil spill on record, experts consider it to be the worst spill in history in terms of the damage done to the environment.[1]

Of course Exxon, the company that owned the ship, also paid a price. Their representatives estimate that the incident cost the company $3.5 billion:

- $2.2 billion in cleanup costs

- $300 million in claims paid

- $1 billion in state and federal settlements[2]

But that's not all. In addition to what Exxon has already paid, they stand to lose an additional $5 billion in punitive damages, a judgment they are still attempting to reverse through the appellate process more than a decade after the incident.

What was the cause of such an expensive and far-reaching accident? The answer can be found in the *Law of the Chain*.

When the *Exxon Valdez* cast off from the Alyeska Pipeline Terminal on the evening of March 23, the voyage began routinely. An expert ship's pilot guided the vessel through the Valdez Narrows and then returned control of the ship to its captain, Joe Hazelwood. The captain ordered that the ship be put on a particular course, turned control over to Third Mate Gregory Cousins, and left the bridge. Thirty-five minutes later, the *Exxon Valdez* was stranded on a reef and leaking tons of oil into the sea.

Investigation following the accident painted an ugly picture: neglect of safety standards, indifference to company policy, and unwise decision making. The ship's captain had been drinking during the hours before he took command of the ship. One officer, rather than the required two, remained in the wheelhouse as the tanker navigated the Valdez Narrows, and again after the pilot left the ship. And that officer, Cousins, had been so overworked that fatigue is thought to have contributed to the navigation error that followed. Nor was a lookout always present on the bridge while the vessel was underway.

There were also discrepancies between what Captain Hazelwood told the Vessel Traffic Center he was doing, and the orders he actually gave on the ship. At 11:30 P.M. the captain radioed that he would take a course of 200 degrees and reduce speed to wind his way through the icebergs that sometimes float in the shipping lanes. Yet the engine logs showed that the ship's speed kept increasing. Nine minutes after that, the captain ordered that the ship take a course of 180 degrees and be put on autopilot, but he never informed the traffic center of the change. Then, at 11:53, he left the bridge.

At four minutes after midnight, the ship was on the reef. For almost two hours, first Cousins and then Hazelwood tried to get the ship free, which was all the while leaking oil into the sea. In the first three hours, an estimated 5.8 million gallons of oil poured out from the distressed tanker. By then the damage was done, and the weak link had caused the "chain" to break. Alaska's coastline was a mess, Hazelwood's career as a ship captain was over, and Exxon was stuck with a public-relations nightmare and massive financial obligations.

OBSERVE

As much as any team likes to measure itself by its best people, the truth is that the strength of the team is impacted by its weakest link. No matter how much people try to rationalize it, compensate for it, or hide it, a weak link will eventually come to light.

1. When you hear about Exxon on the news or pass an Exxon station, do you ever think about the spill in 1989?

   _____ Yes _____ No

2. What were some of the damages to the environment made by the spill?

_____

_____

_____

3. Who was responsible for the *Exxon Valdez* spill? Why?

_____

_____

_____

4. How did the actions of the crew affect the entire company?

_____

_____

_____

5. In your industry or area of service, what group or organization has suffered by ignoring the *Law of the Chain?* How does this group reflect the idea that the strength of the team is impacted by its weakest link?

_____

_____

_____

LEARN

One of the mistakes I often made early in my career as a team leader was that I thought everyone who was on my team should remain on the team. That was true for several reasons. First, I naturally see the best in people. When I look at individuals with potential, I see all that they can become—even if they don't see it themselves. And I try to encourage and equip them to become better. Second, I truly like people. I figure that the more people who take the trip, the bigger the party. Third, because I have vision and believe my goals are worthwhile and beneficial, I sometimes naively assume that everyone will want to go along with me.

But just because I wanted to take everyone with me didn't mean that it would always work out that way. From my experiences, I've discovered that when it comes to teamwork . . .

1. Not Everyone *Will* Take the Journey

Some people don't want to go for personal reasons. For other people the issue is their *attitude*. They don't want to change, grow, or conquer new territory. They hold fast to the status quo. All you can do with people in this group is kindly thank them for their past contributions and move on.

2. Not Everyone *Should* Take the Journey

Other people shouldn't join a team because of their *agenda*. They have other plans, and where you're going isn't the right place for them. The best thing you can do for people in this category is wish them well, and as far as you are able, help them on their way so that they achieve success in their venture.

3. Not Everyone *Can* Take the Journey

For the third group of people, the issue is *ability*. They may not be capable of keeping pace with their teammates or helping the group get where it wants to go. How do you recognize people who fall into this category? They're not very hard to identify. Often they

- Can't keep pace with other team members.

- Don't grow in their areas of responsibility.

- Don't see the big picture.

- Won't work on personal weaknesses.

- Won't work with the rest of the team.

- Can't fulfill expectations for their areas.

If you have people who display one or more of these characteristics, you need to acknowledge that they are weak links.

If you have people on your team who are weak links, you really have only two choices: Train them or trade them. Of course, your first priority should always be to try to train people who are having a hard time keeping up. Help can come in many forms: giving people books to read, sending them to conferences, giving them new challenges, pairing them up with mentors. I believe that people often rise to your level of expectations. Give them hope and training, and they usually improve.

But what should you do if a team member continually fails to meet expectations, even after receiving training, encouragement, and opportunities to grow? My father used to have a saying: "Water seeks its own level." Somebody who is a weak link on your team might be capable of becoming a star on another team. You need to give that person an opportunity to find his or her own level somewhere else.

If you are a team leader, you cannot avoid dealing with weak links. Team members who don't carry their own weight not only slow down the team, they impact your leadership. Take a look at some of the things that happen when a weak link remains on the team.

1. The Stronger Members Identify the Weak One

A weak link cannot hide (except in a group of weak people). If you have strong people on your team, they always know who isn't performing up to the level of everyone else.

2. The Stronger Members Have to Help the Weak One

If your people must work together as a team in order to do their work, then they have only two choices when it comes to a weak teammate: They can ignore the person and allow the team to suffer, or they can help him or her and make the team more successful. If they are team players, they will help.

3. The Stronger Members Come to Resent the Weak One

Whether strong team members help or not, the result will always be the same: resentment. No one likes to lose or fall behind because of the same person.

4. The Stronger Members Become Less Effective

When you're carrying someone else's load in addition to your own, it compromises your performance. Do this for a long time, and the whole team suffers. A weak link always eventually robs the team of momentum—and potential.

5. The Stronger Members Question the Leader's Ability

Finally, any time the leader allows a weak link to remain a part of the team, the team members forced to compensate for the weak person begin to doubt the leader's courage and discernment. You lose the respect of the best when you don't deal properly with the worst.

If your team has a weak link who can't or won't rise to the level of the team—and you've done everything you can to help the person improve—then you've got to take action. Take the advice of authors Danny Cox and John Hoover. If you need to remove somebody from the team, be discreet, be clear, be honest, and be brief. Then once the person is gone, be open about it with the rest of the team while maintaining respect for the person you let go.[3] And if you start to have second thoughts before or afterward, remember this: As long as a weak link is part of the team, everyone else on the team will suffer.

✧ EVALUATE ✧

Rate your own teamwork abilities by placing the number 1, 2, or 3 next
to each of the following statements:

1 = Never   2 = Sometimes   3 = Always

_____   1. When I recruit volunteers, I understand that not everyone will want to be a part of the team.

_____   2. I can tell you who my team members believe is the weak link on our team.

_____   3. I can distinguish between the people I should ask to join my team and the people I should not ask to join my team.

_____   4. I don't take it personally when someone declines my offer of becoming part of a team that I am heading up.

_____   5. A weak link will pull down the other members of the team.

_____   6. As a team member, I try to help the weak link on my team.

_____   7. As a leader, I understand that the weak link will affect my entire team.

_____   8. When I discover a weak link, I work to train or trade him or her.

_____   9. I can easily identify the weaker members of the team.

_____   10. When a weak link is eliminated from my team, I do not bring up that person's weaknesses or faults in future conversations with my team members.

_____   **Total**

24 – 30   This is an area of strength. Continue growing, but also spend time helping others to develop in this area.

16 – 23   This area may not be hurting you, but it isn't helping you much either. To strengthen your teamwork ability, develop yourself in this area.

10 – 15   This is an area of weakness in your teamwork. Until you grow in this area, your team effectiveness will be negatively impacted.

✑ DISCUSS ✑

Answer the following questions and discuss your answers when you meet with your team.

1. What are some reasons that people have given for not joining your team? How did you react?

   _____

   _____

   _____

   _____

   _____

2. How do you recognize the people who will hinder your team?

   _____

   _____

   _____

   _____

3. Why is it important to identify the weaker members of your team?

   _____

   _____

   _____

   _____

4. When you identify a weak link on your team, how do you react?

   _____

   _____

   _____

5. In the past, how has your organization dealt with weak links? Did you agree with the decisions that were made?

_____

_____

_____

_____

_____

6. As a leader, how would you approach the weak link on your team? What would be your responsibility in this situation?

_____

_____

_____

_____

_____

7. What does your organization or team need to do to strengthen its "chain"?

_____

_____

_____

_____

_____

8. What do you need to do to avoid becoming the weak link?

_____

_____

_____

_____

_____

TAKE ACTION

Most people's natural inclination is to judge themselves according to their best qualities, while they measure others by their worst. As a result, they point to areas where their teammates need to grow. But the truth is that every person is responsible for his or her own growth first.

Take a hard look at yourself. Using the criteria from the *Law of the Chain*, examine yourself to see where you may be hindering the team. Mark the box under the word *Self* for any issue that applies to you. And if you have real courage, ask your spouse or a close friend to evaluate you by marking the boxes listed under the word *Friend*.

Evaluated by		Possible Issues
Self	*Friend*	
❑	❑	*Have trouble keeping pace with other team members.*
❑	❑	*Am not growing in my area of responsibility.*
❑	❑	*Have a hard time seeing the big picture.*
❑	❑	*Have difficulty seeing my personal weaknesses.*
❑	❑	*Have a tough time working with the rest of the team.*
❑	❑	*Consistently fail to fulfill expectations in my area of responsibility.*

If you (or the other person who evaluated you) checked more than one box, you need to put yourself on a growth plan so you don't hinder your team. Talk to your team leader or a trusted mentor about ways you can grow in any weak area.

6

THE LAW OF
THE CATALYST

Winning Teams Have Players Who Make Things Happen

⚜ READ ⚜

Most teams don't naturally get better on their own. Left alone, they don't grow, improve, or reach championship caliber. Instead, they tend to wind down. The road to the next level is always uphill, and if a team isn't intentionally fighting to move up, then it inevitably slides down. The team loses focus, gets out of rhythm, decreases in energy, breaks down in unity, and loses momentum. At some point it also loses key players. And it's only a matter of time before it plateaus and ultimately declines into mediocrity. That's why a team that reaches its potential always possesses a catalyst!

Catalysts are what I call *get-it-done-and-then-some* people. The greatest catalyst I've ever had the privilege of seeing in action is Michael Jordan. In the opinion of many people (including me), he is the greatest basketball player ever to play the game, not only because of his talent, athleticism, and understanding of the game, but also because of his ability to perform as a catalyst. His résumé as an amateur and as a professional with the Chicago Bulls attests to that ability:

- Won NCAA Division One championship (1982)

- Twice named the *Sporting News* College Player of the Year (1983 and 1984)

- Received the Naismith and Wooden Awards (1984)

- Won two Olympic gold medals (1984 and 1992)

- Won six NBA world championships (1991, '92, '93, '96, '97, '98)

- Selected NBA Rookie of the Year in 1985

- Selected to the NBA All-Rookie team (1985)

- Selected for All-NBA First Team a record 10 times (1987, '88, '89, '90, '91, '92, '93, '96, '97, '98)

- Holds the NBA record for highest career scoring average (31.5 points per game)

- Holds the NBA record for most seasons leading the League in scoring (10)

- Holds the NBA record for most seasons leading the League in field goals made (10) and attempted (10)

- Ranks third in NBA history in points (29,277), third in steals (2,306), and fourth in field goals (10,962)

- Voted NBA Defensive Player of the Year in 1988 (after being criticized that he was only an offensive player)

- Selected to the All NBA Defensive First Team 9 times (1988, '89, '90, '91, '92, '93, '96, '97, '98)

- Named NBA most valuable player (MVP) 5 times (1988, '91, '92, '96, '98)

- Named NBA finals MVP 6 times (1991, '92, '93, '96, '97, '98)

- Named one of the 50 greatest players in NBA history

Statistics make a strong statement about Jordan, but they really don't tell the whole story. For that, you had to see him in action. When the Bulls needed to get the team out of a slump, the ball went to Jordan. When a player needed to take the last shot to win the game, the ball went to Jordan. Even if the team needed to get things going in practice, the ball went to Jordan. No matter what the situation was on the court, Jordan was capable of putting the team in the position to win the game. That's always the case for championship teams. Winning teams have players who make things happen.

Even when Michael Jordan retired from basketball as a player he was still in the game. In early 2000, Jordan became part owner and president of basketball operations of the Washington Wizards. Only a week after becoming part of the organization, Jordan put on a number 23 Wizards jersey and joined the team for a practice.

Wizards forward Tracy Murry, who guarded Jordan during some drills, remarked afterward, "He's definitely moving the same way . . . dunking the ball, shooting a jump shot, fade away. Still got the same game, hasn't gone anywhere."

Nobody expected his talent to diminish, especially not just two years after his retirement. But his ability as a catalyst hadn't diminished either. Murry continued, "And as soon as he sets foot in that gym, he starts talking trash, so of course the intensity is going to pick up."

Intensity is what every catalyst brings to the table. One commentator remarked of Jordan's visit to the court, "By being himself, he turned a Wizards practice into something it hasn't been in a while—energetic and fun."

"Which is what we should expect every day," was Jordan's reaction. "Actually, I told them they shouldn't have to wait for me to come out to show the energy that they had today. I just tried to keep them focused, challenge them, say whatever I have to say. If they can play hard against me, they can play hard against anybody. It was fun."[1]

That's the way it always is for a catalyst. Fun. Stirring up the team, making things happen, doing whatever it takes to push the team to the next level is what they love. When a catalyst does this consistently, the team becomes expectant, confidant, elevated, and, ultimately, amazed.

❦ OBSERVE ❦

When crunch time comes, a catalyst becomes critical, whether it's the salesperson who hits the "impossible" goal, the ballplayer who makes the big play, or the parent who gets a child to believe in him- or herself at a critical moment in life. A team can't reach big goals or even break new ground if it doesn't have a catalyst.

1. How would you describe Michael Jordan?

    _____

    _____

    _____

    _____

    _____

    _____

2. What makes Michael Jordan a catalyst?

3. How does a team benefit from having a catalyst?

4. Who are the catalysts in your industry or area of service? What makes them catalysts?

✍ LEARN ✍

My experience with teams has taught me that what is true for sports is also true for relationships in business, ministry, and family. When the clock is running down and the game is on the line, there are really only three kinds of people on a team:

- **People who don't want the ball:** Some people don't have the ability to come through for the team in high-pressure situations, and they know it. As a result, they don't want the responsibility of carrying the team to victory. And it shouldn't be given to them. They should simply be allowed to play in their areas of strength.

- **People who want the ball but shouldn't have it:** A second group contains people who can't carry the team to victory. The problem is that they *don't* know that they can't. Often these players' egos are greater than their talent. Such people can be dangerous to a team.

- **People who want the ball and should get it:** The final group, which is by far the smallest, consists of people who want to be "go-to" players at crunch time and who can actually deliver. They are able to push, pull, or carry the team to new levels when the going gets tough. These are the catalysts.

Every team needs catalysts if it wants to have any hope of winning consistently. Without them, even a team with loads of talent cannot go to the highest level.

It's easy to point out a team's catalyst after he or she has made an impact on the group and spurred them on to victory, especially in the world of sports. But how do you recognize a catalyst before the fact? How do you find catalytic people for your current team?

No matter what kind of "game" you're playing or what kind of team you're on, you can be sure that catalysts have certain characteristics that make them different from their teammates. I've observed nine traits that are often present in the catalysts with whom I've interacted:

1. Intuitive

Catalysts sense things that others don't sense. They may recognize a weakness in an opponent. They may smell an opportunity that others don't. They may be able to make an intuitive leap that turns a disadvantage into an advantage. Whatever it is they sense, they are able to use this ability to help the team succeed.

2. Communicative

Catalysts say things that other team members don't say, in order to get the team moving. Sometimes they do it to share with their teammates what they have sensed intuitively, so that they will be better prepared to meet the challenge. Other times their purpose is to inspire or incite other team members. And they usually know the difference between when a teammate needs a boost—and when he needs a boot.

3. Passionate

Catalysts feel things that others don't feel. They are passionate about what they do, and they want to share that love with their teammates. Sometimes the passion explodes as a controlled fury to achieve goals in their areas of passion. Other times it manifests itself as a contagious enthusiasm. However it comes out, it can inspire a team to success.

4. Talented

Catalysts are capable of doing what others cannot. That's because their talent is as strong as their passion. People rarely become catalysts outside an area of expertise and gifting. That's the case for two main reasons. First, talent knows what it takes to win. You can't take the team to the next level when you haven't mastered the skills it takes to succeed on a personal level. It just doesn't happen.

The second reason is that part of being a catalyst is influencing other team members. You can't do that if you have no credibility because of your own poor performance. Part of being a catalyst is sharing your gift with others to make them better. You can't give what you don't have.

5. Creative

Another quality commonly found in catalysts is creativity. Catalysts think things that others do not think. While most team members may do things by rote (or by rut), catalysts think differently from their teammates. They are constantly looking for fresh, innovative ways to do things.

6. Initiating

I enjoy creative people, and I've worked with many through the years. In fact, I consider myself to be creative, especially in the areas of writing and teaching. But my experience with creative people has taught me something about them: While all creative people have more than enough ideas, not all of them are good at implementing those creative thoughts.

Catalysts don't have this problem. They do things that others cannot do. Not only are they creative in their thinking, they are disciplined in their actions. They delight in making things happen. So they initiate. And as a result, they move the team as they move themselves.

7. Responsible

Catalysts carry things that others do not carry. My friend Truett Cathy, founder of Chik-fil-A, has a saying: "If it's to be, it's up to me." That could very well be the motto for all catalysts. Catalysts are not consultants. They don't recommend a course of action; they take responsibility for making it happen.

8. Generous

Catalysts give things that others don't give. One of the true marks of people's taking responsibility is their willingness to give of themselves to carry something through. Catalysts display this quality. They are prepared to use their resources to better the team, whether this means giving time, spending money, sacrificing personal gain, or something else.

9. Influential

Finally, catalysts are able to lead teammates in a way that others cannot. Team members will follow a catalyst when they won't respond to anyone else. In the case of a highly talented team member who is not especially gifted in leadership, he or she may be an effective catalyst in an area of expertise. But people with natural leadership ability will have influence far beyond their own team.

Michael Jordan, again, is a wonderful example. Obviously he had influence with his teammates in Chicago. But his influence stretched far beyond the Bulls. I got a taste of that firsthand at the NBA All-Star game. I had the pleasure of speaking to the players and officials at the chapel before the game, and later I got to spend time with the referees who had been picked to officiate. During my talks with them, I asked what player they respected the most in terms of his honesty. Their answer was Michael Jordan.

One of the refs then recounted that in a close game, Danny Ainge, whose team was playing against the Bulls, made a shot near the three-point line. The officials had given Ainge only two points for the basket, since they were not sure if he was outside the three-point line. During the time-out immediately after the shot, one of the refs asked Jordan whether his opponent's score had been a valid three-point shot. Jordan indicated that it was. They gave Ainge the three points. Jordan's integrity—and influence—caused them to reverse their call.

When you see many of those nine qualities in someone on your team, take heart. When crunch time comes, he or she is likely to step up to a whole new level of performance, and attempt to take the team there too.

❧ EVALUATE ❧

Rate your own teamwork abilities by placing the number 1, 2, or 3 next to each of the following statements:

1 = Never   2 = Sometimes   3 = Always

_____	1. I can recognize the times when I need to be thrown the ball.
_____	2. I know how I can best help the team.
_____	3. I am intuitive in my profession or area of service and can sense things that others don't sense.
_____	4. I communicate direction and encouragement to the members of my team.
_____	5. I am passionate about what I do, and I want to share that excitement with the members of my team.
_____	6. I know what it will take to win, and I am prepared to perform at that level.
_____	7. People tell me that I make things happen in ways others can't.
_____	8. Once I have an idea, I take the necessary steps to put that idea in motion.
_____	9. I take responsibility for my actions and know that "if it's to be, it's up to me."
_____	10. I have influence beyond my stated position.
_____	**Total**

24 – 30   This is an area of strength. Continue growing, but also spend time helping others to develop in this area.

16 – 23   This area may not be hurting you, but it isn't helping you much either. To strengthen your teamwork ability, develop yourself in this area.

10 – 15   This is an area of weakness in your teamwork. Until you grow in this area, your team effectiveness will be negatively impacted.

✿ DISCUSS ✿

Answer the following questions and discuss your answers when you meet with your team.

1. What is a catalyst?

   _____

   _____

   _____

   _____

   _____

2. How can you identify the catalysts in your organization?

   _____

   _____

   _____

   _____

   _____

   _____

   _____

3. How can you or your team's leader approach a person who thinks he or she should be the catalyst for the team, but doesn't have the strength to take the team to the next level?

   _____

   _____

   _____

   _____

   _____

4. What are some challenges your team might face when a catalyst steps up and takes charge? How can these challenges be dealt with in a positive way?

_____

_____

_____

_____

_____

5. What do you need to do in order to create a team that embraces catalysts?

_____

_____

_____

_____

6. In what areas are you capable of stepping up and being a catalyst when needed?

_____

_____

_____

_____

TAKE ACTION

How are you when it comes to crunch time on your team? Do you want the ball, or would you rather it were in someone else's hands? If there are more talented and effective catalysts on your team, then you should not want to be the go-to player in a pinch. In those cases, the best thing you can do is get an "assist" by helping to put those people in position to benefit the team. But if you avoid the spotlight because you are afraid or because you haven't worked as hard as you should to improve yourself, then you need to change your mind-set.

Start to put yourself on the road to improvement by doing the following things:

1. *Find a mentor.* Players become catalysts only with the help of people more skilled than themselves. Find someone who makes things happen to help you along the way.

2. *Begin a growth plan.* Put yourself on a program that will help you develop your skills and talents. You cannot take the team to a higher level if you haven't gotten there.

3. *Get out of your comfort zone.* You won't know what you're capable of until you try to go beyond what you've done before.

If you follow these three guidelines, you still may or may not become a catalyst, but you will at least become the best you can be—and that's all that anyone can ask of you.

7

THE LAW OF
THE COMPASS

Vision Gives Team Members Direction and Confidence

✤ READ ✤

For nearly a hundred years, IBM has been a rock of American business, standing firm in the stream of competition. Even during the depression of the 1930s, while thousands of companies were disappearing, IBM kept growing. The source of its strength was business and technological innovation.

For half a century, IBM continually broke ground in the area of computers, beginning in the 1940s with its Mark I. In the 1950s and 1960s, IBM introduced innovation after innovation. By 1971, it was receiving $8 billion in annual revenue and employed 270,000 people. When people thought of blue-chip companies, IBM is likely whom they pictured.

But for all its history of advances, by the late 1980s and early 1990s, the company was struggling. For a decade IBM had been slow to react to technological changes. As a result, by 1991, it suffered $8 billion in *losses* every year. And even though IBM fought to regain ground technologically, consumer perception of the company was at an all-time low. Where IBM had once been seen as dominant, people now looked upon it as hopelessly behind the times—a slow-moving dinosaur among new companies that moved like cheetahs. If something didn't change, IBM was going to be in big trouble.

Then, in 1993, IBM got a new CEO, Lou Gerstner. He quickly began recruiting key members for his team, IBM's executive committee. Perhaps the most important addition was Abby Kohnstamm, whom he invited to be IBM's senior vice president of marketing.

Kohnstamm was eager to get started. She believed the company's products were strong enough, but that its marketing was weak. When she arrived at IBM, what she found was much worse than she had expected. Not only was IBM failing to reach customers effectively; when it came to the marketing department, employees weren't even sure who did what, or why. For example, when Kohnstamm asked how many employees were in the marketing area, she couldn't get the same answer from any two employees. Greg Farrell of *USA Today* described the situation: "The company was a fragmented, decentralized organization with more than a dozen quasi-autonomous businesses, and seventy ad agency partners worldwide."[1]

Kohnstamm immediately dismissed all those agencies and hired one to replace it: Ogilvy & Mather Worldwide. Her desire was to give the entire IBM team a single unifying theme for the hardware, software, and services they had to offer. Before long, she had found it. The company adopted the concept of "e-business." Kohnstamm asserts, "E-business is the single focal point for the company, and is the single largest marketing effort ever undertaken by IBM."[2]

The vision seems to be working. Steve Gardner, an ad agency owner who once promoted Compaq, says, "The most stunning thing about e-business was that it transformed IBM from perceived laggard to leader in the Internet space without any real change in its lines of products or services. That's an astonishing achievement."[3]

Where once IBM was struggling, it now has renewed direction and confidence. Bill Etherington, senior vice president and group executive over sales and distribution, says that the marketing focus has had an incredibly positive effect on IBM's employees. And he should know. He's been with IBM for thirty-six years. He says, "We all had enthusiasm for this wonderful campaign. It had an edge to it and portrayed the company in a much more modern light."[4] Maureen McGuire, vice president of marketing communications, agrees: "The campaign has galvanized employees. We're trying to get all those people to sing the same song, read from the same book."

For a company that hadn't sung for a long time, that's a great achievement. And it just goes to show you, vision gives team members direction and confidence. That's the power of the *Law of the Compass.*

✐ OBSERVE ✐

Great vision precedes great achievement, and every team needs a compelling vision to give it direction. A team without vision is, at worst, purposeless. At best, it is subject to the personal agendas of its various teammates. As the agendas work against each other, the team's energy and drive drain away. On the other hand, a team that embraces a vision becomes focused, energized, and confident. It knows where it's headed and why it's going there.

1. What was the history of IBM before Lou Gerstner joined the team?

   _____

   _____

   _____

   _____

2. Describe the marketing department at IBM when Kohnstamm first arrived.

   _____

   _____

   _____

   _____

3. Why did Kohnstamm fire the seventy ad agencies and hire only one to represent IBM?

   _____

   _____

   _____

   _____

4. What did the concept of e-business do for the employees of IBM?

   _____

   _____

   _____

   _____

   _____

   _____

5. Who is the model for the *Law of the Compass* in your industry or area of service? How is he or she using a single vision to give the team members direction and confidence?

_____

_____

_____

_____

_____

⌦ LEARN ⌦

Have you ever been part of a team that didn't seem to make any progress? Maybe the group had plenty of talent, resources, and opportunities, and team members got along, but the group just never *went* anywhere! If you have, there's a strong possibility that the situation was caused by lack of vision.

Field Marshal Bernard Montgomery, a great leader of troops during World War II who was called a "soldier's general," wrote that "every single soldier must know, before he goes into battle, how the little battle he is to fight fits into the larger picture, and how the success of his fighting will influence the battle as a whole." People on the team need to know why they're fighting. Otherwise, the team gets into trouble.

If you lead your team, then you will need to identify a worthy and compelling vision and articulate it to your team members. However, even if you are not the leader, identifying a compelling vision is still important. If you don't know the team's vision, you can't perform with confidence. You can't be sure you and your teammates are going in the right direction. You can't even be sure that the team you're on is the right one for you if you haven't examined the vision in light of your strengths, convictions, and purpose. For everyone on the team, the vision needs to be compelling!

How do you measure a vision? How do you know whether it is worthy and compelling? You check your compass. Every team needs one. In fact, every team needs several compasses. Take a look at the following six "compasses." The team should examine each one before it embarks on any kind of journey.

A team's vision must be aligned with a

1. Moral Compass (Look Above)

Millionaire philanthropist Andrew Carnegie exclaimed, "A great business is seldom if ever built up, except on lines of strictest integrity." That holds true for any endeavor. There's only one true north. If your compass is pointing in any other direction, your team is headed the wrong way.

A moral compass brings integrity to the vision. It helps all the people on the team check their motives and make sure they are laboring for the right reasons. It also brings credibility to the leaders who cast the vision—but only if they model the values that the team is expected to embrace. When they do, they bring fuel to the vision, which keeps it going.

2. Intuitive Compass (Look Within)

Where integrity brings fuel to the vision, passion brings fire. And the true fire of passion and conviction only comes from within.

In *The Leadership Challenge* (Jossey-Bass Publishers, 1987), James Kouzes and Barry Posner explain that "visions spring forth from our intuition. If necessity is the mother of invention, intuition is the mother of vision. Experience feeds our intuition and enhances our insight." A vision must resonate deep within the leader of the team. Then it must resonate within the team members who will be asked to work hard to bring it to fruition. But that's the value of that intuitive passion. It brings the kind of heat that fires up the committed—and fries the uncommitted.

3. Historical Compass (Look Behind)

There's an old saying that I learned when I lived in rural Indiana: "Don't remove the fence before you know why it's there." You never know—there might be a bull on the other side! A compelling vision should build on the past, not diminish it. It should make positive use of anything contributed by previous teams in the organization.

Any time you cast vision, you must create a connection between the past, the present, and the future. You must bring them together. People won't reach for the future until they have touched the past. When you include the history of the team, the people who have been in the organization a long time sense that they are valued. (Even if they are no longer the stars.) At the same time, the newer people receive a sense of security, knowing that the current vision builds on the past and leads to the future.

What is the best way to do this? You tell stories. Principles may fade in people's minds, but stories stick. They bring relationships to the vision. Tell stories from the past that give a sense of history. Tell stories about the exciting things that are happening now among team members. And tell the story of what it will be like the day that the team fulfills the vision. Stories are like thumbtacks that help to keep a vision in front of people.

4. Directional Compass (Look Ahead)

Henry David Thoreau wrote, "If one advances confidently in the direction of his dreams, and endeavors to live the life which he has imagined, he will meet with success unexpected in common hours." As I already mentioned, vision provides direction for the team. Part of that direction comes from a sense of purpose. Another comes from having goals, which bring targets to the vision.

A goal serves as great motivation to the team. NFL referee Jim Tunney commented on this when he said, "Why do we call it a goal line? Because eleven people on the offensive team huddle for a single purpose—to move the ball across it. Everyone has a specific task to do—the quarterback, the wide receiver, each lineman—every player knows exactly what his assignment is. Even the defensive team has its goals—to prevent the offensive team from achieving its goal."

5. Strategic Compass (Look Around)

A goal won't do the team much good without steps to accomplish it. Vision without strategy is little more than a daydream. As Vince Abner remarked, "Vision isn't enough—it must be combined with venture. It is not enough to stare up the steps; we must step up the stairs."

The value of a strategy is that it brings process to the vision. It identifies resources and mobilizes the members of the team. People need more than information and inspiration. They need instruction in what to *do* to make the vision become reality and a way to get there. A strategy provides that.

6. Visionary Compass (Look Beyond)

Finally, the vision of the team must look beyond current circumstances and any obvious shortcomings of current teammates to see the potential of the team. A truly great vision speaks to what team members can become if they truly live out their values and work according to their highest standards.

If you are your team's leader, getting people to reach their potential means challenging them. As you know, it's one thing to have team members *show* up. It's another to get them to *grow* up. One of the things about a far-reaching vision is that it brings "stretch" to the team.

Without a challenge, many people tend to fall or fade away. Charles Noble observed, "You must have a long-range vision to keep you from being frustrated by short-range failures." That's true. Vision helps people with motivation. That can be especially important for highly talented people. They sometimes fight lack of desire. That's why a great artist like Michelangelo prayed, "Lord, grant that I may always desire more than I can accomplish." A visionary compass answers that prayer.

Someone once said that only people who can see the invisible can do the impossible. This shows the value of vision. But it also indicates that vision can be an elusive quality. If you can confidently measure the vision of your team according to these six "compasses," and you find them all aligned in the right direction, then your team has a reasonably good chance at success. And make no mistake. Not only can a team not thrive without vision—it cannot even survive without it. The words of King Solomon of ancient Israel, reputed to be the wisest man who ever lived, are true: "Where there is no vision, the people perish."[5] Vision gives team members direction and confidence—two things they cannot do without.

❧ EVALUATE ❧

Rate your own teamwork abilities by placing the number 1, 2, or 3 next to each of the following statements:

1 = Never   2 = Sometimes   3 = Always

_____   1. I follow the guidelines made by the leaders of my organization.

_____   2. My actions are reflective of my own moral integrity.

_____   3. I have a passion for the work I do.

_____   4. I am knowledgeable about the history of my organization and who the key players are.

_____   5. My goals for my team build upon our past successes.

_____   6. I have a sense of purpose, which aligns with the work I do and the goals I set.

_____   7. Once I set a goal, I take time to develop a strategy for reaching it.

_____   8. I can look beyond our current circumstances to see the ultimate potential of our team.

_____   9. I do not get frustrated with setbacks. I keep moving forward.

_____   10. I have written down my vision for my team.

_____   **Total**

24 – 30   This is an area of strength. Continue growing, but also spend time helping others to develop in this area.

16 – 23   This area may not be hurting you, but it isn't helping you much either. To strengthen your teamwork ability, develop yourself in this area.

10 – 15   This is an area of weakness in your teamwork. Until you grow in this area, your team effectiveness will be negatively impacted.

✑ DISCUSS ✑

Answer the following questions and discuss your answers when you meet with your team.

1. Why is it important for your team to have compasses?

   _____

   _____

   _____

   _____

   _____

2. Describe your team's *moral compass*.

   _____

   _____

   _____

   _____

3. Describe your team's *intuitive compass*.

   _____

   _____

   _____

   _____

4. Describe your team's *historical compass*.

   _____

   _____

   _____

   _____

5. Describe your team's *directional compass*.

_____

_____

_____

6. Describe your team's *strategic compass*.

_____

_____

_____

7. Describe your team's *visionary compass*.

_____

_____

_____

8. Who is responsible for setting your team's compass? How is the compass set?

_____

_____

_____

_____

9. What can you do to make sure you are aligned with your organization's compasses?

_____

_____

_____

_____

TAKE ACTION

What is the vision for your team? You'd be surprised how many individuals are part of a group that works together but isn't clear about why. A team can't move forward in confidence if it has no compass!

As a member of your team, you need a clear understanding of its vision. If the team doesn't have one, then help it develop one. If the team has already found its compass and course, then you need to examine yourself in light of it to make sure there is a good match. If there isn't, both you and your teammates are going to be frustrated. And everyone will probably be best served by a change.

In the space below, write out your team's vision. If your team doesn't have a defined vision, work to develop one with the members of your team.

_____

_____

_____

_____

_____

_____

_____

_____

_____

_____

_____

_____

_____

Find somewhere in your work area to post your team's vision as a reminder to yourself and your coworkers. Everything you do should work to fulfill this vision.

8

THE LAW OF THE BAD APPLE

Rotten Attitudes Ruin a Team

⤷ READ ⤶

Growing up, I loved basketball. It all started for me in the fourth grade when I saw a high school basketball game for the first time. I was captivated. Soon after that my dad poured a cement driveway along the side of our house and put a goal up on the garage for me. From that day until I went to college, I could usually be found practicing my shooting and playing pickup games on that small home court.

By the time I got to high school, I had become a pretty good player. I started on the junior varsity team as a freshman, and when I was a sophomore, our JV team had a 15-3 record, which was better than that of the varsity. We were proud of that—maybe a little too proud. I say this because of something that happened during my junior year.

Critics who followed high school basketball in Ohio thought our team had a chance to win the state championship in our division. I guess they looked at the players who would return as seniors from the previous year's varsity team and saw the talent that would be moving up from the JV, and they figured we would be a powerhouse. And we did have a lot of talent. How many high school teams in the late 1960s could say that all but a couple of players on the team could dunk the ball? But the season turned out far different from everyone's expectations.

From the beginning of the season, the team suffered problems. There were two of us juniors on the varsity who had the talent to start for the team: John Thomas, who was the team's best rebounder, and me, the best shooting guard. We thought playing time should be based strictly on ability, and we figured we deserved our places on the team. The seniors, who had taken a backseat to the previous year's seniors, thought we should be made to pay our dues and wait.

What began as a rivalry turned into a war between the juniors and the seniors. When we scrimmaged at practice, it was the juniors against the seniors. In games, the seniors wouldn't pass to the juniors and vice versa. We even judged our success not by whether the team won or lost, but by whether the juniors' stats were better than the seniors'. If we outshot, outpassed, and outrebounded the seniors, then we thought we had "won" the game, regardless of the outcome against our opponent.

The battles got to be so fierce that before long, the juniors and the seniors wouldn't even work together on the court during games. Coach Neff had to platoon us. The seniors would start, and when a substitution became necessary, he'd put not one but *five* juniors in the game. We became two teams on one roster.

I don't remember exactly who started the rivalry that split our team, but I do remember that John Thomas and I embraced it early on. I've always been a leader, and I did my share of influencing other team members. Unfortunately, I have to confess that I led the juniors in the wrong direction.

What started as a bad attitude in one or two players made a mess of the situation for everyone. By the time we were in the thick of our schedule, even the players who didn't want to take part in the rivalry were affected. The season was a disaster. In the end, we finished with a mediocre record and never came close to reaching our potential. It just goes to show you, bad attitudes ruin a team.

✆ OBSERVE ❧

One of the things I learned through my high school basketball experience is that talent is not enough to bring success to a team. Of course, you do need talent. My friend Lou Holtz, the outstanding college football coach, observed, "You've got to have great athletes to win . . . You can't win without good athletes, but you can lose with them." But it also takes much more than talented people to win. It takes talented people with the right attitude.

1. Describe the attitude of the players on my high school basketball team.

    _____

    _____

    _____

2. What was the goal for the juniors and seniors?

    _____

    _____

    _____

    _____

3. What should have been the goal for the team?

_____

_____

_____

_____

_____

4. How did the attitudes of the players get in the way of reaching their potential as a team?

_____

_____

_____

_____

_____

5. What team in your industry or area of service has suffered from bad attitudes? How has a rotten attitude ruined their team?

_____

_____

_____

_____

_____

❧ LEARN ☙

My high school team was loaded with talent, and if that were enough we could have been state champions. But our team was also loaded with bad attitudes. You know which won the battle between talent and attitude in the end. Perhaps that is why, to this day, I understand the importance of a positive attitude and have placed such a strong emphasis on it for myself, for my children as they were growing up, and for the teams I lead.

Years ago I wrote something about attitude in my book *The Winning Attitude:*

> Attitude . . .
>
> It is the "advance man" of our true selves.
>
> Its roots are inward, but its fruit is outward.
>
> It is our best friend or our worst enemy.
>
> It is more honest and more consistent than our words.
>
> It is an outward look based on past experiences.
>
> It is a thing which draws people to us or repels them.
>
> It is never content until it is expressed.
>
> It is the librarian of our past.
>
> It is the speaker of our present.
>
> It is the prophet of our future.[1]

Good attitudes among players do not guarantee a team's success, but bad attitudes guarantee its failure.

Read the following five truths about attitudes and how they affect a team, and I think you will recognize how attitude makes a major impact on teamwork.

1. Attitudes Have the Power to Lift Up or Tear Down a Team

In *The Winner's Edge*, Dennis Waitley stated, "The real leaders in business, in the professional community, in education, in government, and in the home also seem to draw upon a special cutting edge that separates them from the rest of society. The winner's edge is not in a gifted birth, in a high IQ, or in talent. The winner's edge is in the attitude, not aptitude."

Unfortunately, I think many people resist that notion. They want to believe that talent alone (or talent with experience) is enough. But there are plenty of talented teams out there who never amount to anything because of the attitudes of their players.

Take a look at how various attitudes impact a team made up of highly talented players:

Abilities	+	Attitudes	=	Result
Great Talent	+	Rotten Attitudes	=	Bad Team
Great Talent	+	Bad Attitudes	=	Average Team
Great Talent	+	Average Attitudes	=	Good Team
Great Talent	+	Good Attitudes	=	Great Team

If you want great results, you need good people with great talent *and* awesome attitudes. When attitudes go up, so does the potential of the team. When attitudes go down, the potential of the team goes with it.

2. An Attitude Compounds When Exposed to Others

There are a lot of things on a team that are not contagious: Talent. Experience. Practice. But you can be sure of one thing: Attitude is catching. When someone on the team is teachable and his humility is rewarded by improvement, others are more likely to display similar characteristics. When a leader is upbeat in the face of discouraging circumstances, others admire that quality and want to be like that person. When a team member displays a strong work ethic and begins to have a positive impact, others imitate him or her. People become inspired by their peers. People have a tendency to adopt the attitudes of those they spend time with—to pick up on their mind-sets, beliefs, and approaches to challenges.

A wonderful example of the way attitudes often "compound" can be seen in the story of Roger Bannister. During the first half of the twentieth century, many sports experts believed that no runner could run a mile in less than four minutes. And for a long time they were right. But then on May 6, 1954, British runner and university student Roger Bannister ran a mile in 3 minutes, 59.4 seconds during a meet in Oxford. Less than two months later, another runner, Australian John Landy, also broke the four-minute barrier. Then suddenly dozens and then hundreds of others broke it. Why? Because the best runners' attitudes changed. They began to adopt the mind-set and beliefs of their peers.

Bannister's attitude and actions compounded when exposed to others. His attitude spread. Today, every world-class runner who competes at that distance can run a mile in less than four minutes. Attitudes are contagious!

3. Bad Attitudes Compound Faster than Good Ones

There's only one thing more contagious than a good attitude—and that's a bad attitude. For some reason, many people think it's chic to be negative. I suspect that they think it makes them look smart or important. But the truth is that a negative attitude hurts rather than helps the person who has it. And it also hurts the people around him.

A wise old baseball manager once remarked that he never allowed the positive players to room with the negative ones on the road. When he created the team's room assignments, he always put the negative ones together so that they couldn't poison anyone else.

4. Attitudes Are Subjective, So Identifying a Wrong One Can Be Difficult

Have you ever interacted with someone for the first time and suspected that his or her attitude was poor, yet you were unable to put your finger on exactly what was wrong? I believe many people have that kind of experience.

The reason people doubt their observations about others' attitudes is that attitudes are subjective. Someone with a bad attitude may not do anything illegal or unethical. Yet that person's attitude may be ruining the team just the same.

People always project on the outside how they feel on the inside. Attitude is really about how a person feels. That overflows into how he or she acts. Allow me to share with you six common rotten attitudes that ruin a team, so that you can recognize them for what they are when you see them.

- An inability to admit wrongdoing

- Failing to forgive

- Petty jealousy

- Putting oneself before the team

- A critical spirit

- A desire to hog all the credit

Certainly there are other negative attitudes that I haven't named, but my intention isn't to list every bad attitude—just some of the most common ones. In a word, most bad attitudes are the result of selfishness. If one of your teammates puts others down, sabotages teamwork, or makes himself out to be more important than the team, then you can be sure that you've encountered someone with a bad attitude.

5. Rotten Attitudes, Left Alone, Ruin Everything

Bad attitudes should never be left unaddressed. You can be sure that they will always cause dissension, resentment, combativeness, and division on a team. And they will never go away on their own if they are left unaddressed. They will simply fester and ruin a team—along with its chances for reaching its potential.

Because people with bad attitudes are so difficult to deal with and because attitudes seem subjective, you doubt your own gut reaction when you encounter a "bad apple." After all, if it's only your *opinion* that he or she has a bad attitude, then you have no right to address it, right? Not if you care about the team. Rotten attitudes ruin a team. That is always true. If you leave a bad apple in a barrel of good apples, you will always end up with a barrel of rotten apples.

❧ EVALUATE ❧

Rate your own teamwork abilities by placing the number 1, 2, or 3 next to each of the following statements:

1 = Never   2 = Sometimes   3 = Always

_____	1. I am aware that my attitude is my choice.
_____	2. People make comments about my positive attitude.
_____	3. When I have made an error, I promptly admit my mistake.
_____	4. When offered a sincere apology, I will fully forgive the other person and will not hold a grudge.
_____	5. I'm not perfect, so I don't expect other people to be perfect.
_____	6. I treat everyone kindly but differently, according to their personalities and interests. This allows my interaction to be more personal.
_____	7. I don't expect life to be fair.
_____	8. My actions reflect the *Law of Significance* instead of my own self-importance.
_____	9. It makes me feel good to share the credit with my team members and know that we've accomplished something together.
_____	10. I try to associate with people who have positive attitudes and who will help to keep my attitude in check.

_____   **Total**

24 – 30   This is an area of strength. Continue growing, but also spend time helping others to develop in this area.

16 – 23   This area may not be hurting you, but it isn't helping you much either. To strengthen your teamwork ability, develop yourself in this area.

10 – 15   This is an area of weakness in your teamwork. Until you grow in this area, your team effectiveness will be negatively impacted.

✑ DISCUSS ✑

Answer the following questions and discuss your answers when you meet with your team.

1. From your own experience, how has a bad attitude (either your own or someone else's) affected a project that you worked on?

   _____

   _____

   _____

   _____

   _____

2. Why is it important to have the right attitude when working with a team?

   _____

   _____

   _____

   _____

   _____

3. How does your team deal with people whose attitudes are bad?

   _____

   _____

   _____

   _____

   _____

   _____

4. How can you counter the bad attitude of another team member?

_____

_____

_____

_____

_____

_____

5. How can you keep your own attitude in check?

_____

_____

_____

_____

_____

_____

TAKE ACTION

The first place to start when it comes to attitude is with yourself. How are you doing when it comes to attitude? For example, do you . . .

❑ think the team wouldn't be able to get along without you?

❑ secretly (or not-so-secretly) believe that recent team successes are *really* attributable to your personal efforts—not the work of the whole team?

❑ keep score when it comes to the praise and perks handed out to other team members?

❑ have a hard time admitting when you make a mistake? (If you believe you're not making mistakes, you need to check this box!)

❑ bring up past wrongs from your teammates?

❑ believe that you are being grossly underpaid?

If you checked any of the above boxes with a "yes," then you need to check your attitude.

Talk to your teammates and find out if your attitude is doing damage to the team. Talk to your leader. And if you really think your pay is inequitable, you need to talk it out with your employer and find out where you really stand. Anytime a relationship is unequal, it cannot last—whether you are giving more than you get or getting more than you deserve. In either case, the relationship will break down.

THE LAW OF COUNTABILITY

*Teammates Must Be Able to Count on Each Other
When It Counts*

ᘓᕙ READ ᕙᘐ

One of the things I like about Atlanta, Georgia, where I moved my family and my companies in 1997, is that it's a sports town. I don't get the chance to go to a lot of games, but there are few things I like better than attending a sporting event. The energy and excitement of watching a team in competition, with a friend or two, is a joy—whether it's the Braves (baseball), the Hawks (basketball), the Falcons (football), or the Thrashers (hockey).

When it was announced that Atlanta would be getting a hockey team, plans were made to build the team a new arena. The old Omni, where the Hawks had played since the early 1970s, was slated to be demolished and replaced on the same site by the Philips Arena. It would be an 18,000-seat, state-of-the-art entertainment complex with box seating, which could host not only hockey and basketball but also concerts and other events.

Tearing down the Omni wasn't going to be a simple process. First, it needed to be done quickly so that construction could begin on the new arena. Second, because the old structure had a cantilevered roof, taking the building apart in opposite order from the way it was constructed was out of the question. It would be far too dangerous for the demolition crews. That left only one choice: blowing it up.

When demolition crews need help blowing up a building—or more accurately, imploding a building—they inevitably turn to the Loizeaux family, the people who pioneered the safe demolition of buildings using explosives. They are owners and founders of Controlled Demolition Incorporated (CDI). The company was founded by Jack Loizeaux, who started a company in the 1940s removing tree stumps with dynamite. In 1957, he blasted his first building. And in the 1960s he began CDI. Since that first demolition—an apartment building in Washington, D.C.—his company has demolished more than 7,000 structures worldwide.

CDI is a family operation. Jack and his wife, Freddie, ran the business in the beginning. It wasn't long before they were joined by their sons, Mark and Doug. When Jack retired in 1976, his sons began running the operation. Today they are joined by several of Mark's children, including daughter Stacey, who has worked in the field since age fifteen and is already an expert in her own right.

When the Loizeauxs were contacted for the Omni job, they quickly discovered that it wouldn't be easy because of its proximity to other buildings. On one side was the World Congress Center, which is used for conventions. On another side was a station for MARTA (Atlanta's mass-transit rail system). On the third was the CNN Center, from which cable and radio programming broadcasts twenty-four hours a day. And CNN Plaza was a mere thirteen feet away from the Omni! A mistake could damage the MARTA line and shut it down at one of its busiest stations. Or it could put the CNN news service temporarily out of business. And, of course, in a worst-case scenario, the Omni could topple in the wrong direction and take down the CNN building itself. It would take every bit of the Loizeauxs' expertise and fifty years of experience to do the task right.

Using explosives to take down a building is always a dangerous undertaking. Each project is unique and requires a custom-made strategy. Holes are drilled in strategic places in many parts of the structure, such as in columns, and filled with appropriate amounts of explosive material. Then those blast points are often wrapped in chain-link fence (to catch the big pieces upon detonation) and then wrapped in a special fabric that helps contain the explosion. "It allows the concrete to move, but it keeps the concrete from flying," says Stacey Loizeaux. "We also sometimes put up a curtain around the entire floor, to catch stuff that gets through these first two layers. That's really where your liability is."[1] Often, earthen berms are also erected around the building to protect nearby people and structures.

Obviously there is risk anytime someone works with explosives. But the greatest danger comes in the way explosives are rigged to go off. To get the building to fall in on itself, the Loizeauxs and their crew have to precisely sequence the charges, often using delays that differ from one another by the tiniest fractions of a second. That was the case for the Omni, where first the roof needed to fall straight down, then three of the walls would need to fall inward, and then the fourth wall outward. And on July 26, 1997, at 6:53 A.M., that's exactly the way it happened. The demolition took ten seconds.

When it comes to blowing up a building the way the Loizeauxs do, everything has to go right—from the analysis of the building, to the planning of the demolition, to the transportation of the explosives, to the rigging of those devices, to the preparation of the building for the safety of the surrounding area. If anyone on the crew fails to get his or her part right and lets the other members of the team down, not only does the CDI team fail in its objective, but it also puts a lot of people and property in danger. When it counts, teammates must be able to count on each other.

❦ OBSERVE ❧

The importance of the *Law of Countability* is clearest when the stakes are high. But you don't have to be in an explosive situation for the law to come into play. If there is a breakdown in countability, then the account is lost, the customer goes away unhappy, or the job goes to some other candidate. Teammates must be able to count on each other when it counts.

1. What made the Omni a uniquely challenging job for CDI?

   _____

   _____

   _____

2. What steps were taken before the day of the blast?

   _____

   _____

   _____

3. Why was it important that every member of the team did his or her job correctly?

   _____

   _____

   _____

   _____

   _____

4. How does the *Law of Countability* factor into your life? When have you had to depend on your family, friends, or coworkers?

_____

_____

_____

5. What team in your industry or area of service models the *Law of Countability*? How do they ensure that they will be able to count on each other when it counts?

_____

_____

_____

 LEARN

I believe that there is a formula for countability. It's not complicated, but its impact is powerful. Here it is:

Character + Competence + Commitment + Consistency + Cohesion = Countability

When all team members embrace each of those five qualities, within themselves and with one another, they can achieve the countability necessary for a team to succeed.

Let's spend some time looking at each quality:

1. Character

In *The 21 Irrefutable Laws of Leadership*, I wrote about the *Law of Solid Ground*, which says that trust is the foundation of leadership. That law is really about character. "Character makes trust possible. Trust makes leadership possible. That is the *Law of Solid Ground.*"[2]

In a similar way, countability begins with character because it is based on trust, which is the foundation for all interaction with people. If you cannot trust someone, you will not count on him. As Robert A. Cook remarked, "There is no substitute for character. You can buy brains, but you cannot buy character."

Anytime you desire to build a team, you have to begin by building character in the individuals who make up the team. Barry Gibbons, in his book *This Indecision Is Final,* asserted, "Write and publish what you want, but the only missions, values, and ethics that count in your company are those that manifest themselves in the behavior of all the people, all the time."[3]

2. Competence

I spent over twenty-five years as a pastor, so I understand the church world very well, and I must admit that there are people in the religious community who act as if character is the only thing that matters. I don't think that's true. What you do is also important (as Scripture makes clear).[4] Character is the most important thing, but it's not the only thing.

If you have any doubts about that, consider this: If you had to go into surgery because of a life-threatening illness, would you be happier having a good surgeon who was a bad person or a good person who was a bad surgeon? That puts it in perspective, doesn't it? Competence matters. And if the person is going to be on the same team with you, you want both competence *and* character.

3. Commitment

Having fair-weather team members doesn't make for a very pleasant team experience. When times are tough, you want to know that you can *count* on your teammates. You don't want to be wondering whether they're going to hang in there with you.

Recently Dan Reiland shared with me the following table that indicates the commitment of various team members.

Level	Type of Teammate	Description
1. Green Beret Colonel	Committed Team Leader	Dedicated to the Cause. Focused on the big picture. Has a whatever-it-takes attitude.
2. First Lieutenant	Team Achiever	Buys into the spirit and culture of the organization. Is self-motivated and productive.
3. OCS Graduate	Genuine Team Player	Has passion and enthusiasm. Arrives early and stays late. Is not yet a proven leader.
4. Private	Formal Team Member	Enjoys being on the team. Wants to stay. Serves out of duty. Not yet a high achiever.
5. Boot Camp Recruit	Begrudging Follower	Will work, but only with a kick in the seat of the pants.
6. Deserter	Nonfollower	Won't do anything. Needs to be court-martialed.
7. Sniper	Dangerous Follower	Works, but makes life difficult for team. Will shoot teammates if given the chance.

Teams succeed or fail based on teammates' commitment to one another and the team. My friend Randy Watts, who pastors a church in Virginia, sent me a note recently after a conference where I taught the *Law of Countability*. He wrote,

> Years ago, a friend of mine attended the Virginia Military Institute, known for its rugged physical, mental, and emotional training. He told me that all the incoming freshmen are separated into companies. One of their training obstacles is to race up House Mountain, which is very steep and more than a challenge. The motivation for climbing: If you finish last, you run again. Not you, but your whole company! This makes for team commitment. If a person in your company twists an ankle or breaks a leg, other members of his company carry him! It is not enough to be the first man on top of the mountain; everyone on the team has to make it.

That's the kind of commitment that real teamwork requires. When teammates can't make it, you carry them the rest of the way for the sake of the team.

4. Consistency

Every once in a while somebody comes along who defines consistency for the rest of his teammates. In the case of the Atlanta Braves, I believe that person is Greg Maddux. If you follow baseball, then you probably know about him. Maddux is a great pitcher and he has the awards—and statistics—to prove it. He's won more than 200 games, including 176 games in the 1990s, the most of any pitcher in major-league baseball. He is the only pitcher besides Cy Young and Gaylord Perry to have won fifteen or more games in thirteen consecutive sea-

THE LAW OF COUNTABILITY

sons. He is the only pitcher in baseball's history to have won the Cy Young Award four years in a row (1992–1995).

For all of Maddux's awards for pitching and great stats, do you know what has been his most remarkable honor? He has been recognized as the National League's best fielder in his position by receiving a Golden Glove *ten years in a row!*

Many great pitchers are not known for their fielding. When a difficult ball is hit to a pitcher, or when the pitcher has to cover first base on a tough play to the right side of the infield, many times the other players on the team hold their breath. If anyone on the field is likely to make a fielding mistake, it's the pitcher. But not Maddux. He works at his fielding with the same dedicated work ethic that has made him a great pitcher. The result is a career that has seen only forty errors in fifteen years (with two seasons of error-free fielding).

If you want your teammates to have confidence in you, where they know they can count on you day in and day out, then make someone like Maddux your example. Consistency is key.

5. Cohesion

The final quality that teammates need to develop countability is cohesion. That's the ability to hold together no matter how difficult the circumstances get. Navy SEAL John Roat describes cohesion this way:

> Unit cohesion is one of those terms that everyone thinks they understand. In truth, most people don't have a clue. It is definitely not about everybody liking each other or being nice. It means you have a pride in the ability of your group to function at a higher level than possible for the individual. The unit doesn't shine because you're a member, you shine because you're good enough to be a member.[5]

There's an old saying when it comes to teams: "Either we're pulling together or we're pulling apart." Without cohesion, people aren't really a team, because they're not pulling together. They're merely a group of individuals working for the same organization.

When it comes down to it, countability is being able to have faith in your teammates, no matter what happens. When the chips are down, you can turn to the people on your team. Let's face it: You can't do anything that counts unless you have countability.

❦ EVALUATE ❧

Rate your own teamwork abilities by placing the number 1, 2, or 3 next to each of the following statements:

1 = Never   2 = Sometimes   3 = Always

_____   1. I keep my word. When I say I'll do something, I do it.

_____   2. I care about the members of my team without expectations. My words and actions do not have ulterior motives.

_____   3. I perform my job to the best of my ability.

_____   4. I have a whatever-it-takes attitude, and will not give up when things get hard.

_____   5. People know what to expect from me because my work is consistent.

_____   6. I have pride in the ability of my group, and confidence that together we can achieve great things.

_____   7. I do not lie or mislead the members of my team, even if the truth might be unflattering to me.

_____   8. I trust my teammates and don't try to do everything myself.

_____   9. I am self-motivated and productive.

_____   10. When someone on my team breaks trust with me or with the entire group, I talk to that person one-on-one and try to improve the situation.

_____   **Total**

24 – 30   This is an area of strength. Continue growing, but also spend time helping others to develop in this area.

16 – 23   This area may not be hurting you, but it isn't helping you much either. To strengthen your teamwork ability, develop yourself in this area.

10 – 15   This is an area of weakness in your teamwork. Until you grow in this area, your team effectiveness will be negatively impacted.

✑ DISCUSS ✑

Answer the following questions and discuss your answers when you meet with your team.

1. Why is trust among team members important?

   _____

   _____

   _____

   _____

   _____

2. Of the five qualities of countability, in which area does your team excel? Give an example.

   _____

   _____

   _____

   _____

   _____

   _____

3. Which of the five qualities of countability is most important to you? Why?

   _____

   _____

   _____

   _____

   _____

4. What happens when you no longer trust someone?

_____

_____

_____

_____

_____

5. How can your team improve its countability?

_____

_____

_____

_____

_____

6. How can you improve your countability?

_____

_____

_____

_____

_____

TAKE ACTION

People often say that imitation is a compliment. When it comes to teamwork, I believe the highest compliment you can receive is trust from your teammates when it really counts.

How do your teammates feel about you? Do you perform and follow through in such a way that the team considers you someone they can count on? How are you doing in each of the areas examined in the lesson?

This week, go to a person on your team whom you have let down in the past. Confess your error, ask for forgiveness, and make it right.

Also this week, approach a person who has let you down, one-on-one, and try to resolve any lingering mistrust.

The strength of a team lies in its trust among teammates. You need to know for certain that you can count on your teammates, and they need to know that they can count on you.

THE LAW OF
THE PRICE TAG

The Team Fails to Reach Its Potential
When It Fails to Pay the Price

✑ READ ✑

On December 28, 2000, one of the nation's oldest retailers, Montgomery Ward and Company, announced that it would be filing Chapter 7 bankruptcy and closing its doors forever. That announcement saddened the people of Chicago, for Ward's had been an institution in that city for more than a century. Even sadder is that their failure might have been avoided if they had learned and practiced the *Law of the Price Tag* before it was too late.

The retailing chain's early history is really quite remarkable. The company was founded in 1872 by Aaron Montgomery Ward, a young salesman who had worked for various dry goods merchants throughout the Midwest and South. While he was working in rural areas far from cities or large towns, he discovered that many consumers in remote areas were at the mercy of local merchants who often overcharged them for merchandise. This gave him an idea. Railroads and mail service were greatly improving by that time. What if he bought dry goods directly from manufacturers for cash and sold them for cash via mail order to rural consumers, thus eliminating the middlemen who were gouging those customers?

In 1871, Ward saved enough money from his work as a salesman to purchase some merchandise and print a one-page price list that he planned to mail out to a bunch of farmers who belonged to a fraternal organization. But before he could follow through with his plan, the great Chicago fire of 1871 destroyed his stock and price sheets. That didn't stop Ward. He convinced two sales colleagues to join him as partners, began rebuilding his stock, and reprinted the price sheet, which would become the world's first general merchandise mail-order catalog. And in 1872, at age twenty-eight, Ward opened for business.

At first, Ward was only moderately successful. In fact, a year into the business, his two partners got cold feet and asked to be bought out. Ward paid them off, then took his friend George Thorne into the business as a full partner. Together they worked hard, taking orders and shipping out merchandise by rail. Meanwhile, in 1875, Ward and Thorne came up with a novel idea. They decided to include a new credo in their catalog: "Satisfaction Guaranteed or Your Money Back." And the business began to take off.

Ward's tenacity and willingness to pay the price twice for starting his own business came to fruition less than a decade later. The company that had begun with $1,600 of capital in 1872 had sales of $300,000 in 1878. Nine years after that, the company's sales rose to $1 million. By the turn of the century, Montgomery Ward and Company's catalog, which would come to be known as the "Wish Book," grew to five hundred pages and was being mailed to more than a million people every year. And the company's headquarters was a new building on Michigan Avenue in Chicago—the biggest skyscraper west of New York City.[1]

Then, in 1901, Montgomery Ward retired in order to spend the final years of his life working to make Chicago a better place. During the first two decades of the new century, the company continued to thrive. But in the late 1910s, things began to change. Ward's success had prompted the start of another Chicago-based company in 1886: Sears, Roebuck, and Company. It, like Montgomery Ward and Company, was a catalog-based merchant that catered to rural customers. Back when both companies began business, most of the United States' population lived in rural areas. But now the country was changing. Cities were filling up. When the 1920 census was completed, it showed that for the first time in the nation's history, the majority of the population lived in urban centers—and shopping habits were changing as a result.

Robert E. Wood, a former army quartermaster general, was brought in to run Montgomery Ward in 1919, and he saw the coming boom in retail sales. He wanted to begin opening stores in cities where people could shop in person, but he couldn't get the owners to do it.[2] They simply would not pay the price to make the change.

Knowing where the future lay in the business, Wood left Ward's. In 1924, he went on staff at Sears as vice president. He convinced the people who ran Sears to take a chance on retail store sales. They agreed to open one store in Chicago as a test the following year. It was an immediate success. Two years later, Sears had opened 27 stores. By 1929, the company had built over 300. Even during the Depression, they continued to expand, and in 1931 Sears' retail store sales surpassed their catalog sales.[3] Wood became the company's chairman, a position he held until 1954, and Sears became the most successful department store chain in the country.

Montgomery Ward and Company never really recovered from that early error. It began opening retail stores, but it wasn't aggressive enough to overtake Sears. A team fails to reach its potential when it fails to pay the price. Time after time, Ward failed to pay the price. During the Depression, the company hoarded cash and stopped expansion while Sears gained more ground. After World War II, when other stores began moving to the suburbs, Ward failed to seize the opportunity to try to get back on top. Each time the market changed, they didn't pay the price necessary to win a market. For the last twenty-five years, they've struggled to keep their doors open. Finally, after 128 years in business, they closed. That's what can happen when people violate the *Law of the Price Tag*.

✨ OBSERVE ✨

If a team doesn't reach its potential, seldom is the issue ability. It's rarely a matter of resources either. It's almost always a payment issue. Montgomery Ward and Company had plenty of resources, and it had the talent it needed—including the leader who could move the team forward. The problem was that the company's owners were unwilling to get out of their comfort zone, take a risk, and break new ground.

1. Describe the time when Montgomery Ward was successful.

   _____

   _____

   _____

2. What happened to derail the success of Montgomery Ward?

   _____

   _____

   _____

3. Why did Robert E. Wood leave Montgomery Ward?

_____

_____

_____

4. In what ways did Sears pay the price to move ahead of the competition?

_____

_____

_____

5. Has Sears continued to pay the price?

_____

_____

_____

6. What team in your industry or area of service is the model for the _Law of the Price Tag?_ What price did they pay to reach their potential?

_____

_____

_____

_____

7. What team in your industry or area of service failed to reach its potential when it didn't pay the price? What was the price? What reward did they miss?

_____

_____

_____

❧ LEARN ❧

One of the reasons teams fail to pay the price to reach their potential is that they misunderstand the *Law of the Price Tag*. They honestly don't know how it works. Allow me to give you four facts about this law that will help to clarify it in your mind:

1. The Price Must Be Paid by Everyone

In *Straight Talk for Monday Morning*, Allan Cox observed,

> "You have to give up something to be a member of a team. It may be a phony role you've assigned to yourself, such as the guy who talks too much, the woman who remains silent, the know-it-all, the know-nothing, the hoarder of talented subordinates, the non-sharer of some resource such as management information systems (MIS), or whatever. You give up something, to be sure, such as some petty corner of privilege, but you gain authenticity in return. The team, moreover, doesn't quash individual accomplishment; rather it empowers personal contributions."[4]

People who've never had the experience of being on a winning team often fail to realize that *every* team member must pay a price. I think some of them think that if others work hard, they can coast to their potential. But that is never true. If everyone doesn't pay the price to win, then everyone will pay the price by losing.

2. The Price Must Be Paid All the Time

Many people have what I call "destination disease." I describe it in my book *The 21 Indispensable Qualities of a Leader:*

Some people mistakenly believe that if they can accomplish a particular goal, they no longer have to grow. It can happen with almost anything: earning a degree, reaching a desired position, receiving a particular award, or achieving a financial goal.

But effective leaders cannot afford to think that way. The day they stop growing is the day they forfeit their potential—and the potential of their organization. Remember the words of Ray Kroc: "As long as you're green, you're growing. As soon as you're ripe, you start to rot."[5]

Destination disease is as dangerous for a team as it is for any individual. It makes us believe that we can stop working, stop striving, stop paying the price—yet still reach our potential. But as Earl Blaik, former football coach at the United States Military Academy, observed, "There is no substitute for work. It is the price of success." That truth never goes away. That's why President Dwight D. Eisenhower remarked, "There are no victories at bargain prices." If you want to reach your potential, you can never let up.

3. The Price Increases If the Team Wants to Improve, Change, or Keep Winning

Have you ever noticed how few back-to-back champions there are in sports? Or how few companies stay at the top of *Forbes* magazine's lists for a decade? Becoming a champion has a high price. But remaining on top costs even more. And improving upon your best is even more costly. The higher you are, the more you have to pay to make even small improvements. World-champion sprinters improve their times not by seconds, but by hundredths of a second.

No one can move closer to his or her potential without paying in some way to get there. If you want to change professions, you have to get more education, additional work experience, or both. If you want to run a race at a faster pace, you must pay by training harder and smarter. If you want to increase earnings from your investments, you either put in more money or take greater risks. The same principle applies to teams. To improve, change, or keep winning, as a group the team must pay a price, and so must the individuals on it.

4. The Price Never Decreases

Most people who quit don't give up at the bottom of the mountain, they stop halfway up it. Nobody sets out with the purpose of losing. The problem is often a mistaken belief that a time will come when success will suddenly get cheaper. But life rarely works that way.

When it comes to the *Law of the Price Tag*, I believe there are really only two kinds of teams who violate it: those who don't realize the price of success, and those who know the price but are not willing to pay it. No one can force a team member to have the will to succeed. Each member must decide in his or her own heart whether the goal is worth the price that must be paid. But every person ought to know what to expect to pay in order for a team to succeed.

For that reason, I offer the following observations about the cost of being part of a winning team. To become team players, you and your teammates will have at least the following required of you . . .

- **Sacrifice:** There can be no success without sacrifice. James Allen observed, "He who would accomplish little must sacrifice little; he who would achieve much must sacrifice much." When you become part of a team, you may be aware of some of the things you will have to give up. But you can be sure that no matter how much you expect to give for the team, at some point you will be required to give more. That's the nature of teamwork. The team gets to the top only through the sweat, blood, and sacrifice of its team members.

- **Time Commitment:** Teamwork does not come cheaply. It costs you time—that means you pay for it with your life. It takes time to get to know people, to build relationships with them, to learn how you and they work together.

- **Personal Development:** The only way your team will reach its potential is if *you* reach *your* potential. That means today's ability is not enough. Or, to put it the way leadership expert Max DePree did: "We cannot become what we need to be by remaining what we are." That desire to keep striving, to keep getting better, is a key to your own ability, but it is also crucial for the betterment of the team. That is why UCLA's John Wooden, a great team leader and the greatest college basketball coach of all time, said, "It's what you learn after you know it all that counts."

- **Unselfishness:** People naturally look out for themselves. The question "What's in it for me?" is never far from their thoughts. But if a team is to reach its potential, its players must put the team's agenda ahead of their own. And if you give your best to the team, it will return more to you than you give, and together you will achieve more than you can on your own.

Certainly there are other prices individuals must pay to be part of a team. You can probably list several specific ones you've paid to be on a team. The point is that people can choose to stand on the sidelines of life and try to do everything solo. Or they can get into the game by being part of a team. It's a trade-off between independence and interdependence. The rewards of teamwork can be great, but there is always a cost. You always have to *give* up to *go* up.

❦ EVALUATE ❧

Rate your own teamwork abilities by placing the number 1, 2, or 3 next to each of the following statements:

1 = Never   2 = Sometimes   3 = Always

_____	1. I have sacrificed for my team by working overtime.
_____	2. I have invested my own money in resources that will improve my skills.
_____	3. I am committed to a lifetime of personal growth.
_____	4. I am immune to destination disease.
_____	5. More is expected from me as I become more successful.
_____	6. I expect to pay more as I become more successful.
_____	7. I have placed the team's agenda ahead of my own.
_____	8. I read books and take classes to improve my skills.
_____	9. I am aware that if I don't reach my potential, my team will never reach its potential while I'm a member of that team.
_____	10. I expect my sacrifices to pay off.

_____   **Total**

24 – 30   This is an area of strength. Continue growing, but also spend time helping others to develop in this area.

16 – 23   This area may not be hurting you, but it isn't helping you much either. To strengthen your teamwork ability, develop yourself in this area.

10 – 15   This is an area of weakness in your teamwork. Until you grow in this area, your team effectiveness will be negatively impacted.

❦ DISCUSS ❧

Answer the following questions and discuss your answers when you meet with your team.

1. Why does the price have to be paid by everyone on the team?

2. Do you agree that the price will increase as you and your team become more successful? Why or why not?

3. If, as you succeed, the price keeps increasing, then why not just settle for less?

4. What has your team sacrificed to reach a goal?

5. What changes will you need to make to reach your potential?

_____

_____

_____

_____

TAKE ACTION

If you are an achiever, then you probably have lots of dreams and goals. Write down some of the things you desire to accomplish in the next one to five years:

1. _____

2. _____

3. _____

4. _____

5. _____

6. _____

7. _____

8. _____

9. _____

10. _____

Now, which of these goals are you willing to give up? You always need to be ready to ask yourself this question when you are part of a team. When your personal goals conflict with the greater goals of your team, you have three choices:

1. *Put down the goal* (because the team is more important).

2. *Put off the goal* (because it's not the right time).

3. *Part with the team* (because it's better for everyone).

The one thing you have no right to do is expect the team to sacrifice its collective goals for your personal goals.

11

THE LAW OF
THE SCOREBOARD

*The Team Can Make Adjustments
When It Knows Where It Stands*

❧ READ ❧

In the previous chapter you read about Montgomery Ward and Company, a great American business that fell on hard times because it failed to heed the *Law of the Price Tag*. For a couple of decades it looked as if another American institution was headed for a similar disaster: Walt Disney Productions.

The company was of course founded by Walt Disney and his brother Roy in the 1920s. They began by creating silent animation shorts and grew the company into one of the most loved and respected entertainment companies in the world. They continually broke new ground. They produced the first talking cartoon and the first color cartoon, both featuring Mickey Mouse, who has since become an American icon. *Snow White*, the first feature-length animated movie ever, was a radically innovative idea. While it was being made, many called it "Disney's folly."

When it was released in 1937, it became the most successful film ever made up to that time. (Some say it's the most successful of all time!)

During the next two decades, Walt Disney Productions made wonderful movies that became classics. It expanded into television production. And it opened the world's first theme park. The name Disney became synonymous with creative family entertainment.

But after Walt died in 1966, the company started down a very bumpy road. Where Walt Disney Productions had once stood for innovation, it came to be marked by imitation—of its own past successes. Don Bluth, who left Disney in 1979, commented, "We felt like we were animating the same picture over and over again, with the faces changed a little."[1]

Instead of trying to look forward and break ground, Card Walker, who oversaw movie production, always asked himself, "What would Walt have done?" People at the studio began to joke morbidly, "We're working for a dead man."[2] The company continued to crank out formula movies that didn't make a profit, and revenues continued to shrink. In 1981 the film division had an income of $34.6 million. In 1982 its income had fallen to $19.6 million. In 1983 it incurred a loss of $33.3 million. And the value of Disney stock was plummeting.

During that period, many American corporations were becoming victims of hostile takeovers, where Wall Street raiders would gain control of the company, cut it into pieces, and sell off its parts at a profit for themselves and their backers. Since Disney's stock value was down and it carried little debt, it became ripe for a hostile takeover.

In 1984 Disney narrowly avoided one takeover attempt and was facing the threat of yet another when its board of directors finally took a realistic look at where Disney stood. They decided that if the company were to survive, it would require some radical changes, including something it had never done in its history—bringing in someone from outside Disney to run the company.

The people selected to turn Disney around were Michael Eisner, as chairman and CEO, and Frank Wells, as president and COO. Concerning their challenging task, Eisner remarked,

> Our job wasn't to create something new, but to bring back the magic, to dress Disney up in more stylish clothes and expand its reach, to remind people why they loved the company in the first place . . . A brand is a living entity, and it is enriched or undermined cumulatively over time, the product of a thousand small gestures.[3]

Eisner was writing about his work on the Disney brand, but his remarks describe the approach he and Wells took to revitalizing the entire company. That involved a variety of strategies.

For one thing, they changed the name of the organization from Walt Disney Productions to The Walt Disney Company, reflecting the diversity of its interests. They also brought together all the organization's corporate executives and division heads for a weekly lunch to develop cohesiveness and to share ideas across divisions. They hired key leaders, such as Jeffrey Katzenberg, to run their movie and television operations.

In a matter of a few years, Disney once again became a vital player in the entertainment industry. The almost-dead television division produced hits such as *The Golden Girls* and *Home Improvement*. The movie division, which had recently produced few movies and lost so much money, produced more movies in greater volume, with twenty-seven of its first thirty-three turning a profit. Before long, the company had four movie divisions: Disney, Touchstone, Hollywood Pictures, and Miramax.

In late 1987, Disney became the number one studio at the box office for the first time in its history. And the animation division once again began setting the pace for the industry by creating films such as *The Little Mermaid, Beauty and the Beast, Aladdin,* and *The Lion King.*

Eisner and Wells also expanded the company's efforts into new areas. They increased land development and built numerous new hotels at Walt Disney World. In 1987 they opened retail stores in malls for the first time. Four years later they owned 125 stores that were generating $300 million in annual revenue. And, of course, they also improved their theme parks through expansion, innovation, and strategic partnerships with people such as George Lucas and Steven Spielberg. When they took over the company in 1984, the parks were generating $250 million in income. By 1990 their income reached $800 million.

In 2000 The Walt Disney Company had revenues of $25.4 billion, with $2.9 billion in net income (more than double the figures from 1984).[4] Disney has done more than just turn itself around. It has become an entertainment giant and one of the most powerful corporations in the world.

OBSERVE

For many of the years when Disney was struggling, its team members looked at its history and the memory of its dead founder to gauge what to do. What they needed to do was look at the scoreboard. A team can make adjustments when it knows where it stands. Eisner and Wells brought that ability to the company. They understood and implemented the *Law of the Scoreboard.*

1. Why was Disney successful during its early years?

    _____

    _____

    _____

2. Even though Walt Disney was successful when he was alive, why did his team fail to succeed in the years after his death? Why didn't their "What would Walt do?" strategy work?

    _____

    _____

    _____

    _____

3. How did Michael Eisner describe his job at Disney?

    _____

    _____

    _____

4. How did Eisner's and Wells's actions reflect the *Law of the Scoreboard?*

    _____

    _____

    _____

5. What team in your industry or area of service models the *Law of the Scoreboard?* How do they "keep score"? How do they make adjustments?

    _____

    _____

    _____

❧ LEARN ❧

Every "game" has its own rules and its own definition of what it means to win. Some teams measure their success in points scored, others in profits. Still others may look at the number of people they serve. But no matter what the game is, there is always a scoreboard. And if a team is to accomplish its goals, it has to know where it stands. It has to look at itself in light of the scoreboard.

Why is that so important? Because teams that succeed make adjustments in order to continually improve themselves and their situations. For example, look at how a football team approaches a game. Before the competition starts, the team spends a tremendous amount of time planning. Players study hours of game film. They spend days figuring out what their opponent is likely to do, and decide the best way to win. They come up with a detailed game plan.

As the game begins, the game plan is very important and the scoreboard means nothing. But as the game goes on, the game plan means less and less, and the scoreboard becomes more and more important. Why? Because the game is constantly changing. You see, the game plan tells you what you *want* to happen. But the scoreboard tells what *is* happening. No team can ignore the reality of its situation and win.

For any kind of team, the scoreboard is essential in the following ways:

1. The Scoreboard Is Essential to Understanding

In sports, players, coaches, and fans understand the importance of the scoreboard. That's why it is so visible at every stadium, arena, and ball field. The scoreboard provides a snapshot of the game at any given time. Even if you arrive at a game halfway into it, you can look at the scoreboard and assess the situation.

I'm often surprised by how many people outside sports try to succeed without a scoreboard. Some families operate their households without budgets, yet wonder why they are in debt. Some small business owners go year after year without tracking sales or creating a balance sheet, and wonder why they can't grow the business. Some pastors busy themselves with worthy activities, but never stop to measure whether they are reaching people or performing according to biblical standards.

2. The Scoreboard Is Essential to Evaluating

I believe that personal growth is one of the keys to success. That's why I've taught lessons on growth at conferences and in books for more than twenty years. One of the key principles I teach is this:

Growth = Change

I know this sounds overly simple, but people sometimes lose sight of the fact that they cannot grow and remain the same at the same time. Most people are in a position that can be described by something coach Lou Holtz once said: "We aren't where we want to be; we aren't where we ought to be; but thank goodness we aren't where we used to be."

But when it comes to growth, change alone is not enough. If you want to become better, you have to change in the right direction. You can do that only if you are able to evaluate yourself and your teammates. That is another reason for the scoreboard. It gives you continual feedback. Competing without a scoreboard is like bowling without pins. You may be working hard, but you don't really know how you're doing.

3. The Scoreboard Is Essential to Decision Making

Once you've evaluated your situation, you're ready to make decisions. In football, the quarterback uses information from the scoreboard to decide which play to call. In baseball, the scoreboard helps the manager know when to bring in a relief pitcher. In basketball, it can be used to determine whether to call a time-out.

That was the case at Disney. First, Eisner looked at the company to understand its overall position. Then he evaluated individual areas for their effectiveness. Only then was he able to make good decisions concerning how to get Disney back into the game.

4. The Scoreboard Is Essential to Adjusting

The higher the level you and your team are competing on, the smaller the adjustments required to achieve your best. But making key adjustments is the secret to winning, and the scoreboard helps you to see where those adjustments need to be made.

5. The Scoreboard Is Essential to Winning

In the end, nobody can win without the scoreboard. How do you know when the game is on the line without a scoreboard? How do you know when time is running out unless you check the scoreboard? How will you know if it's cruise time or crunch time unless you have the scoreboard as a measuring device? If your desire is to take a leisurely drive with some friends, then you don't need to worry about a thing. But if you're trying to win the Indy 500, then you and your team *must* know how you're doing!

Some organizations see the scoreboard as a necessary evil. Others try to ignore it—something they cannot do for long and still do well in their profession. And some organizations make checking the scoreboard such an important part of their culture that they are continually able to recognize and seize opportunities that lead to huge successes.

✃ EVALUATE ✄

Rate your own teamwork abilities by placing the number 1, 2, or 3 next to each of the following statements:

1 = Never   2 = Sometimes   3 = Always

_____   1. I can name at least three "scoreboards" I use—such as a budget, growth plan, or checklist—to gauge my progress.

_____   2. I write out my goals and the major steps that I will need to take to reach those goals.

_____   3. I encourage honest input from those closest to me so I can better evaluate myself.

_____   4. I will change my habits in order to grow.

_____   5. After I've completed a task, I take time to evaluate my performance. I note the things I did well and the things I can do better in the future.

_____   6. I make decisions after I've evaluated the situation.

_____   7. I have at least one person on whom I depend to hold me accountable for growth. I meet with this person and discuss my personal growth at least once a month.

_____   8. I measure my progress using a "scoreboard" on a daily or weekly basis.

_____   9. I am competitive on a healthy level.

_____   10. I feel a sense of satisfaction when I reach a goal or check off a task on my to-do list.

_____   **Total**

24 – 30   This is an area of strength. Continue growing, but also spend time helping others to develop in this area.

16 – 23   This area may not be hurting you, but it isn't helping you much either. To strengthen your teamwork ability, develop yourself in this area.

10 – 15   This is an area of weakness in your teamwork. Until you grow in this area, your team effectiveness will be negatively impacted.

⋙ DISCUSS ⋘

Answer the following questions and discuss your answers when you meet with your team.

1. Why is it important to have a scoreboard for your team?

   _____

   _____

   _____

2. What types of scoreboards does your team already use? How are these scoreboards helpful to the team?

   _____

   _____

   _____

   _____

3. What other types of scoreboards could your team use?

   _____

   _____

   _____

4. How are you currently measuring your own performance? What new measurement can you add to better evaluate yourself in terms of accomplishing the team's major goals?

   _____

   _____

   _____

5. What is the score? How well is your team performing?

    _____

    _____

    _____

    _____

6. How can you increase your score?

    _____

    _____

    _____

    _____

TAKE ACTION

In order for your team to be successful, each member of the team needs to be clear on how success is measured. Meet one-on-one with your leader and define your scoreboard. Ask how you are being evaluated and ways that you can improve. Set up a time six months from now to see how you've done.

If you are a leader in your group, take some time this week to meet with the members of your team and either review or develop your team's scoreboard. Make sure that whatever you use to keep score is integrally linked to the people of the organization and goals of the team. Look for ways the team can evaluate, adjust, and make decisions based on the scoreboard. Create a system that helps you to consistently and effectively evaluate your scoreboard as a leader and with your team.

12

THE LAW OF
THE BENCH

Great Teams Have Great Depth

ᛉ READ ᛈ

You may have heard the expression, "It's not over until the fat lady sings," or Yogi Berra's famous comment, "It ain't over 'til it's over." Would you believe that sometimes it *is* over before it's over? You can learn to identify such times if you know the *Law of the Bench.*

Let me give you an example. One Saturday in September of 2000, I went to a football game with some friends: Kevin Small, the president of INJOY; Chris Goede, who used to play professional ball; and Steve Miller, my wonderful son-in-law. We were looking forward to an exciting game between the Georgia Tech Yellow Jackets and the Florida State Seminoles, even though FSU was a very strong favorite. There's a pretty good rivalry between all Georgia and Florida college teams, so the teams can get pretty pumped up. And on that day, we weren't disappointed. The teams were battling, and the score was close. Tech was playing its heart out.

But as the third quarter came to a close, I said, "Come on, guys. This one is over."

Now, I sometimes leave games early because I hate to be stuck in traffic. Of course, if a game is really close or is likely to have some historic significance (such as a no-hitter in baseball), I stay to the end. On this day, the guys were a little surprised by my desire to leave, especially since the game was close and Tech had finally pulled ahead, 15 to 12.

"You don't want to see the end of the game?" asked Chris, a little curious.

"No, this game is over," I said. "Let's go to the car."

On our way back, we talked about it. It's true that Tech was hanging in there against FSU, especially when it came to the way the Yellow Jackets were playing defense. That was no easy task because the Seminoles had a powerful offense. But what I had noticed throughout the course of the game was that while Tech's starters were still in the game, FSU had been substituting many players from their bench—and their team's level of play had not been negatively impacted. Because of that, I knew it was only a matter of time before Tech's players would be worn down by the powerful bench of FSU. And sure enough, the game ended with a score of 26 to 21, with FSU on top. That's the impact of the *Law of the Bench*. Great teams have great depth.

OBSERVE

It's not difficult to see the importance of having good reserve players who sit on the bench in sports. A great starter alone is simply not enough if a team wants to go to the highest level. Any team that wants to excel must have good substitutes as well as starters.

1. How was it possible to tell the outcome of the game before the game was over?

   _____

   _____

   _____

   _____

   _____

2. What advantage did Florida State have over Georgia Tech?

   _____

   _____

   _____

   _____

3. Why is a strong bench important in sports?

   _____

   _____

   _____

   _____

4. Why is a strong bench important in your field?

   _____

   _____

   _____

   _____

   _____

5. What team in your industry or area of service uses the *Law of the Bench* to their advantage? How do they use their great depth to their advantage?

_____

_____

_____

_____

_____

_____

❧ LEARN ❧

The *Law of the Bench* is true in any field, not just sports. You may be able to do some wonderful things with just a handful of top people, but if you want your team to do well over the long haul, you've got to build your bench. A great team with no bench eventually collapses.

In sports, it's easy to identify which people are the starters and which make up the bench. But how do you identify them in other fields? I want to suggest the following definitions:

Starters are frontline people who directly add value to the organization or who directly influence its course.

The Bench is made up of the people who add value to the organization indirectly or who support the starters who do.

Everyone recognizes the importance of a team's starters. They are the ones who are most often in the spotlight. As a result, they get most of the credit. And while both groups are important, if one group is liable to be neglected or overlooked, it's usually the people on the bench. In fact, the people most likely to discount or discredit the contribution of the bench may be the starters. Some key players enjoy reminding the substitutes that they are "riding the pine." But any starter who minimizes the contribution of the bench is self-centered, underestimates what it takes for a team to be a success, and doesn't understand that great teams have great depth.

Every human being has value, and every player on a team adds value to the team in some way. Those truths alone should be enough to make team members care about the bench players. But there are also more specific reasons to honor and develop the players who may not be considered "starters." Here are several:

1. Today's Bench Players May Be Tomorrow's Stars

Rare are the people who begin their careers as stars. And those who do sometimes find that their success is like that of some child actors: After a brief flash in the pan, they are never able to recapture the attention they got early on.

Most successful people go through an apprenticeship or period of seasoning. Look at quarterback Joe Montana, who was inducted into the NFL Hall of Fame in 2000. He spent two years on the bench as a backup before being named the San Francisco Forty-niners' starter. And as he was breaking records and leading his team to numerous Super Bowls, the person who sat on the bench as a backup to him was Steve Young, another great quarterback.

Some talented team members are recognized early for their great potential and are groomed to succeed. Others labor in obscurity for years, learning, growing, and gaining experience. Then after a decade of hard work, they become "overnight successes." With the way people like to move from job to job today—and even from career to career—good leaders should always keep their eyes open for emerging talent. Never be in a hurry to pigeonhole someone on your team as a nonstarter. Given the right encouragement, training, and opportunities, nearly anyone who has the desire has the potential to emerge someday as an impact player.

2. The Success of a Supporting Player Can Multiply the Success of a Starter

When every team member fulfills the role that best suits his or her talents, gifts, and experience and excels in that role, then the team really hums. It's the achievement of the whole team that makes the starters flourish, and it's the achievement of the starters that makes the team flourish. The whole team really is greater than the sum of its parts. Or, as John Wooden put it, "The main ingredient of stardom is the rest of the team."

3. There Are More Bench Players Than Starters

If you look at the roster of any successful team, you will see that the starters are always outnumbered by the other players on the team. In professional basketball, twelve people are on the team but only five start. Major-league baseball teams start nine, but carry forty players. In pro football, twenty-two people start on offense and defense, but teams are allowed to have fifty-three players. (College teams often have more than one hundred!)

You find similar situations in every field. In the entertainment industry, the actors are often known, but the hundreds of crew members it takes to make a movie aren't. In ministry, everyone recognizes the people up front during a worship service, but it takes scores of people working behind the scenes to bring that service together. For any politician or corporate executive or big-name fashion designer that you know about, there are hundreds of people working quietly in the background to make their work possible. Nobody can neglect the majority of the team and hope to be successful.

4. A Bench Player Correctly Placed Will at Times Be More Valuable than a Starter

I think if you asked most people how they would classify administrative assistants as team members, they would tell you that they consider them to be bench players, since their primary role is support. I would agree with that—although in some cases administrative people do have direct influence on an organization.

Take for example my assistant, Linda Eggers. Over the years, Linda has done just about everything at INJOY. She has been the company's bookkeeper. She used to run our conferences. She did marketing and product development. She is a very talented person. I think Linda is capable of doing just about anything. But she has chosen to take a supporting role as my assistant. And in that position, she makes a huge impact. Today my company has more than two hundred employees. I respect and value all of them. But if I lost everything tomorrow and could keep only five or six persons with whom to start over from scratch, Linda would be one of the persons I would fight to keep. Her value as a support person makes her a starter.

5. A Strong Bench Gives the Leader More Options

When a team has no bench, the only option its leader has is moving the starters around to maximize their effectiveness. If a starter can't perform, the team is out of luck. When a team has a weak bench, then the leader has a few options, but they are often not very good. But when a team has a great bench, the options are almost endless.

That's why someone like Bobby Bowden, the coach at FSU, was able to wear down Georgia Tech. If one of his players got hurt, he had someone to replace him. If his opponent changed defenses, he had offensive players in reserve to overcome the challenge. No matter what kind of situation he faced, with a strong bench he had options that would give the team a chance to win.

6. The Bench Is Usually Called upon at Critical Times for the Team

When an army is in trouble, what does it do? It calls up the reserves. That's the way it is in every area of life. The time you need the bench isn't when things are going well. It's when things aren't. When the starter gets hurt and the game is in jeopardy, a substitute steps in. That person's effectiveness often determines the team's success.

If your team is experiencing a tough time, then you know the importance of having a good bench. But if you are experiencing a smooth period, then now is time to develop your backup players. Build the bench today for the crisis you will face tomorrow.

❧ EVALUATE ❧

Rate your own teamwork abilities by placing the number 1, 2, or 3 next to each of the following statements:

1 = Never   2 = Sometimes   3 = Always

_____   1. I treat the members of my team with respect, regardless of their roles.

_____   2. I look for the potential in those I work with so I can help to develop their gifts.

_____   3. I am in a role that helps others utilize their talents, gifts, and experience.

_____   4. My leader is able to work on larger tasks because he knows he can count on me to do my part.

_____   5. My achievements help the whole team and reflect well on my leader.

_____   6. I focus my energy on complimenting rather than competing with my team members.

_____   7. The members of my team consider me to be a valuable team member.

_____   8. I keep up-to-date about the major events and projects that my organization takes on.

_____   9. If called upon, I could fill a more demanding role.

_____   10. I take responsibility for my own personal growth.

_____   **Total**

24 – 30   This is an area of strength. Continue growing, but also spend time helping others to develop in this area.

16 – 23   This area may not be hurting you, but it isn't helping you much either. To strengthen your teamwork ability, develop yourself in this area.

10 – 15   This is an area of weakness in your teamwork. Until you grow in this area, your team effectiveness will be negatively impacted.

✿ DISCUSS ✿

Answer the following questions and discuss your answers when you meet with your team.

1. Who are the starters and bench players in your organization?

    _____

    _____

    _____

2. Is there a high turnover with bench players? Why or why not?

    _____

    _____

    _____

3. How do the starters invest in the bench players?

    _____

    _____

4. How can your organization better communicate that every person's role is important?

    _____

    _____

    _____

5. How will you remind the members of your team that they are valuable?

    _____

    _____

    _____

TAKE ACTION

Would you define yourself as a bench player or a starter? Why?

_____
_____
_____

If you are on the bench, then your job is to do two things: help the starters to shine, and prepare yourself to be a starter in the future. You can do this by cultivating an attitude of service and teachability, and by doing whatever you can to learn and grow.

How do you currently display an attitude of teachability and service?

_____
_____
_____

How can you become more proactive in your personal growth?

_____
_____
_____

If you are a starter, then you should not only perform at your best for the sake of the team, but you should also honor the people on the bench. You do this by acknowledging the value of their contributions and by helping prepare them to start some day. If you are not already mentoring a teammate on the bench, start doing so right away.

Who are you mentoring or who will you mentor?

_____
_____
_____

How can you help this person to improve his or her skills?

_____
_____
_____

13

THE LAW OF IDENTITY

Shared Values Define the Team

⚔ READ ⚔

When I moved to Atlanta, I became acquainted with an organization that has developed its own unique identity and fosters a strong sense of team-work despite being a huge company. That organization is The Home Depot.

Now, I am not a do-it-yourselfer. What's the opposite of handy? Handless? Manually challenged? Whatever it is, that's me. Then there's my son, Joel Porter. He never met a tool he didn't like, and if a thing can be fixed, he will find a way to do it. When he was thirteen years old, we let him create a workshop in a room adjacent to our garage. He put in a workbench, installed fixtures, and wired the room. A friend of ours who used to be a contractor said Joel had put enough power in that small room to light up an entire house!

When we arrived in Atlanta, Joel got a job at Home Depot, and he couldn't have been happier. Every day he would come home and tell us about the company, what he did that day, and the values the company held dear.

Intrigued, I did some research of my own. I came to find out that the company was founded by Bernie Marcus and Arthur Blank. They opened their first store in Atlanta in June of 1979, after both men had been fired fourteen months before from Handy Dan, a home improvement chain located in the western part of the United States. For years Marcus, a man with great retail experience and leadership talent, had possessed a vision for a national chain of huge one-stop home improvement stores. His idea was to offer the widest selection of products at the lowest prices with the best customer service possible.

Getting the company off the ground wasn't easy, but they kept plugging away, slowing expanding the business, opening more stores, and attracting first-rate people. Marcus says, "We are only as good as our people—especially the men and women working in our stores every day . . . That's why we believe a sure way of growing this company is to clearly state our values and instill them in our associates."[1]

The right leaders with the right values have attracted the right people to make the company a blockbuster. In 1979 they started with four stores. In 1999 The Home Depot had 775 stores, 160,000 employees, and $38.4 billion in annual sales.[2]

Values truly are at the heart of The Home Depot's success. Marcus explains,

> A set of eight values has been our bedrock for the past twenty years. Although they were not put in writing until 1995, these values—the basis for the way we run the company—enabled us to explode across the North American landscape and will be the vehicle for reaching our ambitious goals in the international marketplace . . .
>
> • Excellent customer service.
>
> • Taking care of our people.

- Developing entrepreneurial spirit.

- Respect for all people.

- Building strong relationships with associates, customers, vendors and communities.

- Doing the right thing, not just doing things right.

- Giving back to our communities as an integral part of doing business.

- Shareholder return.[3]

Those values have made the company a great place for people to work. For example, from the day the first Home Depot opened, the company has offered employees stock options rather than bonuses. This kind of treatment has made more than one thousand of its employees millionaires!

Joel Porter has since left his job at Home Depot. He now works for The INJOY Group™ in a technical capacity as our studio production manager. But he will always have a heart for Home Depot. Why? Because the company has an identity he respects. It has shared values, and those values define their team. That's the impact their organization had on him, and that's the impact the *Law of Identity* can have on you and your team.

❧ OBSERVE ❧

With over 160,000 on the team, it's easy to see that not everyone at Home Depot will share common experiences or have a personal relationship with one another; however, they can still possess a cohesiveness that defies the size of the team. What it takes is a common vision (the *Law of the Compass*) and shared values. The leaders at Home Depot know that if everyone embraces the same values, team members can still have a connection to each other and to the larger team.

1. What was Bernie Marcus's vision?

   _____

   _____

   _____

2. Why is it important to clearly state values to the members of a team?

   _____

   _____

   _____

   _____

3. Why is customer loyalty at the top of Home Depot's list of values?

   _____

   _____

   _____

4. What values similar to those of Home Depot does your organization have?

   _____

   _____

   _____

   _____

5. What team in your industry or area of service models the Law
   of Identity? What are their shared values, and how do they give
   the team definition?

   _____

   _____

   _____

   _____

✤ LEARN ✤

We've all seen teams that have a common goal yet lack common values.
Everyone on the team has different ideas about what's important. The
result is chaos. Eventually the team breaks down if everyone tries to do
things his or her own way. That's why team members need to be on the
same page. Just as personal values influence and guide an individual's
behavior, organizational values influence and guide the team's behavior.

Take a look at how values can help a team to become more connected and more effective. Shared values are like

1. **Glue:** When difficult times come—and they do for every
   team—values are what hold people together. Look at a
   marriage, for example. It's easy for a couple to stay together
   when they are feeling the flush of love and everything is going
   smoothly. But eventually the passion that drew them together
   fades, and adversity comes. What keeps the people who stay
   married together? It's their values. Their values are more
   important than their feelings. They value their marriage so
   highly that they are willing to fight *for* the relationship. If a

couple doesn't have that mind-set going into the wedding, then their chances of staying together are pretty slim. The same is true for any other kind of team. If the players don't know what their values are—and live them out—their chances of working as a unit and reaching their potential are very small.

2. **A Foundation:** All teams need stability to perform well and to grow. Values provide a stable foundation that makes those things possible. This is true for just about any kind of relationship to grow. For example, if you are trying to build a relationship with someone from another culture, you begin by looking for the things you have in common. If you are trying to make a sale with a new customer, you look for common ground. The same is true when it comes to team building. You need something to build on, and values make the strongest foundation.

3. **A Ruler:** Values also help set the standard for a team's performance. In the corporate world, those values are often expressed in a mission statement or set of guidelines for doing business. But sometimes a company's stated values and its real values don't match up.

Author and management expert Ken Blanchard says, "Lots of companies claim they have a set of core values, but what they mean is a list of generic business beliefs that everyone would agree with, such as having integrity, making a profit, and responding to customers. Such values have meaning only when they are further defined in terms of how people actually behave and are rank-ordered to reveal priority." And they function as a measure of expectations and performance when they are genuinely embraced.

---

4. **A Compass:** Do you remember the television show *Dallas* from the 1980s? The main character was J. R. Ewing, a notoriously dishonest businessman. His character code for living can be summarized by something he said in an episode of the show: "Once you give up your ethics, the rest is a piece of cake." To a person with no values, anything goes.

   I think we live in a time when people are searching for standards to live by. When individuals embrace strong values, they possess a moral compass that helps them make decisions. The same is true for people in an organization. When the team identifies and embraces a set of values, then in a month, a year, or a decade, no matter how much circumstances change or what kinds of challenges present themselves, people on the team still know it's moving in the right direction and make good decisions.

5. **A Magnet:** A team's values attract people with like values to the team. In *The 21 Irrefutable Laws of Leadership*, the *Law of Magnetism* states, "Who you are is who you attract." This law is as true for teams as it is for leaders. People attract like-minded people.

6. **An Identity:** Values define the team and give it a unique identity—to team members, potential recruits, clients, and the public. What you believe identifies who you are.

The values of your organization should be unique. Your values should reflect the people on the team and their leader. What's important is that you go through the discovery process and embrace the team's values. Once you do, you will better understand your team, its mission, and its potential.

✐ EVALUATE ✐

Rate your own teamwork abilities by placing the number 1, 2, or 3 next
to each of the following statements:

1 = Never   2 = Sometimes   3 = Always

_____   1. I have personal values that I live by.

_____   2. My personal values coincide with my team's values.

_____   3. I know my team's values.

_____   4. I agree with my team's values.

_____   5. I keep my team's values in mind when making decisions
that will affect or reflect on the team.

_____   6. I know what the leaders of my team expect of me.

_____   7. When I describe my organization to an outsider I include
our values in my description.

_____   8. I communicate the values of our organization with new
members on my team.

_____   9. I commend other people on the team for practicing our
values.

_____   10. I make living my values and the values of the team a
priority, and I take time to compare my actions with those
values to make sure I'm staying on track.

_____   **Total**

24 – 30   This is an area of strength. Continue growing, but also spend time
helping others to develop in this area.

16 – 23   This area may not be hurting you, but it isn't helping you much
either. To strengthen your teamwork ability, develop yourself in
this area.

10 – 15   This is an area of weakness in your teamwork. Until you grow in
this area, your team effectiveness will be negatively impacted.

DISCUSS

Answer the following questions and discuss your answers when you meet with your team.

1. What are your personal values?

   _____

   _____

   _____

   _____

2. What are your team's values? How are they unique to your team or organization?

   _____

   _____

   _____

   _____

   _____

3. How are the values of the organization communicated to you? Who establishes the values? Do the values change? Why or why not?

   _____

   _____

   _____

   _____

   _____

   _____

4. How do the team values impact the team?

_____

_____

_____

_____

_____

5. How can your organization's values be better communicated to the team?

_____

_____

_____

_____

_____

6. What is your incentive for reflecting the team's values?

_____

_____

_____

_____

7. What do you need to do to better reflect the values of your team?

_____

_____

_____

_____

_____

TAKE ACTION

If you've never really thought about how your team's values can reveal its identity and increase its potential, go through the following process with your team:

Articulate the Values. Spend some time thinking about, or bring together a group of key team members to articulate, the team's values. Then put them on paper.

Our team's values are

_____

_____

_____

_____

_____

_____

_____

Compare Values with Practices. Spend time watching the team in action. You want to make sure the values you identify match the ones you're living. When the stated values and the behavior of team members align, it boosts the team's energy and effectiveness. But if they are out of alignment, then the team will suffer.

Examples of how our actions reflect our values:

_____

_____

_____

_____

_____

_____

_____

Examples of how our actions don't align with our stated values:

_____
_____
_____
_____
_____
_____
_____

Teach the Values. Once you've settled on what the right values are, you need to weave those values into your work. Once you are modeling those values, then you can encourage others to incorporate the values into their work.

What I can do to reflect the values of the team:

_____
_____
_____
_____
_____
_____
_____

THE LAW OF COMMUNICATION

Interaction Fuels Action

✑ READ ✑

When Gordon Bethune took over Continental Airlines in 1994, the company was a mess. It had suffered through ten changes in leadership in ten years. It had gone through bankruptcy proceedings twice. Its stock value was at a pitiful $3.25 per share. It had not made a profit in a decade. Customers were flocking away from the airline, and those who did use Continental were rarely happy because, in the words of Bethune, their planes "came and went as they happened to"—with no predictability. That's not what business travelers and vacationers are looking for in an airline!

In his book *From Worst to First*, Bethune described the state of Continental when he arrived:

> In the years leading up to 1994, Continental was simply the worst among the nation's 10 biggest airlines . . . For example, DOT [the

Department of Transportation] measures those 10 largest airlines in on-time percentage . . . *Continental was dead last.* It measures the number of mishandled-baggage reports filed per 1,000 passengers. *Continental was worst.* It measures the number of complaints it receives per 100,000 passengers on each airline. Continental was last. And not just last—in 1994, *Continental got almost three times as many complaints as the industry average* and more than 30 percent more complaints than the ninth-best airline, the runner-up in lousy service. We had a real lock on last place in that category . . . We weren't just the worst big airline. *We lapped the field.*[1]

When a company is that bad, the employees can't help but be affected. Morale at Continental was abysmal. Cooperation was nonexistent. Communication was at an all-time low. Employees had been lied to so often and so thoroughly, they didn't believe anything they were told. According to Bethune, they had learned one survival strategy: Duck. "That's what I joined in 1994," commented Bethune, "a company with a lousy product, angry employees, low wages, a history of ineffective management, and, I soon learned, an incipient bankruptcy, our third, which would probably kill us."[2]

Bethune's goal was to save Continental, but he knew that to do it, he would have to change the culture of the company. The key would be communication. He knew that positive interaction could turn the company around. If he could win the communication battle, he believed he could get the employees to work together again for the good of the team, the customers, and the stockholders.

His first step was to open up the executive offices to the rest of the team. When he began working for Continental, the twentieth-floor suite occupied by top management in Houston was like a fortress. Its doors were locked, the area was surveyed by lots of security cameras, and nobody could enter the area without a proper ID. It wasn't exactly inviting. Bethune literally propped open the doors and hosted open houses for employees to break down the intimidation factor between leadership and the rest of the team.

The next thing he did was work to break the old bureaucracy that had developed over the years. At Continental, rules and manuals had taken the place of communication and the use of judgment. The chief symptom of that mind-set was the nine-inch-thick book of rules for employees that had come to be known as the "Thou Shalt Not" book. It was so detailed that it dictated what color pencil an agent was supposed to use on a boarding pass. In a significant gesture, CEO Bethune, along with Continental president Greg Brenneman, gathered employees in the parking lot, dropped the manual in a trash can, doused it with gasoline, and burned it![3] The message was clear: Everything at Continental was going to change.

Continental didn't change overnight. In fact, as Bethune and Brenneman laid out their "Go Forward Plan," employees were skeptical. But the leaders kept meeting with the people, committed themselves to being honest with them, and maintained their patience. If the news was good, they told the people. If the news was bad, they still told them. They put up bulletin boards in every employee area that showed two things: (1) their ratings for the last year according to the Department of Transportation rating guidelines; and (2) daily news updates from the company. They created a weekly voice-mail message to everyone on the team. They also put lots of communication in writing, using a monthly employee newsletter called *Continental Times and Continental Quarterly,* which they mailed to every employee's home. They put news wire-style LED displays by every coffee and soda machine. They even created 800-number hot lines for questions and information that could be accessed by any employee from anywhere in the world.

A company that had been characterized by distrust and lack of cooperation has become a place where communication is pervasive. Bethune's communication policy is simple: "Unless it's dangerous or illegal for us to share it, we share it."[4] It took time, but eventually the company began to turn. Employees started to trust their leaders. They began to work with and trust one another. And for the first time in more than a decade, the employees of Continental started working as a team.

Today, Continental's service is among the best in its industry. Employee morale is high. And the company is profitable. In 1994, the year Bethune took over, the company *lost* $204 million. In 1995, it made a *profit* of $202 million. The next year its profits doubled. As of April 2001, Continental has posted twenty-four consecutive profitable quarters in an industry where many of its competitors are struggling to stay in the black. The company's stock has split twice, and each share is worth more than ten times the value it had in 1994.

OBSERVE

Communication wasn't the entire reason for Continental's success. But without good communication, the company most likely would have continued on autopilot right into its third (and final) bankruptcy. Creating positive change in an organization requires communication. Interaction fuels action.

1. What communication challenges did Bethune face when he took over Continental?

_____

_____

_____

2. Why was opening the doors to the executive offices a good strategic move?

_____

_____

_____

3. How did Bethune gain his employees' trust?

_____

_____

_____

4. Do you agree with Bethune's policy of "Unless it's dangerous or illegal for us to share it, we share it"? Why?

_____

_____

_____

_____

5. How did open communication help Continental?

_____

_____

_____

6. What team in your industry or area of service models the *Law of Communication?* How do they use interaction to fuel action?

_____

_____

_____

⚜ LEARN ⚜

Only with good communication can a team succeed—it doesn't matter whether that team is a family, a company, a ministry, or a ball club. Effective teams have teammates who are constantly talking to one another. Communication increases commitment and connection, which in turn fuel action. Ironically, if you want your team to *perform* at the highest level, its members need to be able to talk and listen to one another.

If you've ever been on a team where teammates never let each other know what's going on, then you know how frustrating poor communication can be. The team gets stuck because nobody knows what the real agenda is. Important tasks remain uncompleted because certain team members believe other team members are taking care of it—or they duplicate each other's work. Departments within the organization fight because they believe they are being sabotaged by other departments.

In the book *Empowered Teams* (Jossey-Bass Publishers, 1993), authors Richard Wellins, William Byham, and Jeanne Wilson state, "Communication refers to the style and extent of interactions both among members and between members and those outside the team. It also refers to the way that members handle conflict, decision making, and day-to-day interactions."

The success of your team and the ability of your team members to work together depend on good communication. Allow me to give you some guidelines that will help your team to improve in this area. Every team has to learn how to develop good communication in four areas:

1. From Leader to Teammates

The author of *On Leadership,* John W. Gardner, observed, "If I had to name a single all-purpose instrument of leadership, it would be communication." If you are familiar with any of my books on leadership, then you know that I believe everything rises and falls on leadership. What I haven't mentioned before is that leadership rises and falls on communication. If you cannot communicate, you will not lead others effectively.

If you lead your team, give yourself three standards to live by as you communicate to your people:

- **Be Consistent.** Nothing frustrates team members more than leaders who can't make up their minds. One of the things that won the team to Gordon Bethune was the consistency of his communication. His employees always knew they could depend on him and what he said.

- **Be Clear.** Your team cannot execute if they don't know what you want. Don't try to dazzle anyone with your intelligence; impress them with your simple straightforwardness.

- **Be Courteous.** Everyone deserves to be shown respect, no matter what their position or what kind of history you might have with them. If you are courteous to your people, you set a tone for the entire organization.

Never forget that as the leader, your communication sets the tone for the interaction among your people. Teams are a reflection of their leaders. But good communication is never one-way. It should not be top-down or dictatorial. Good leaders listen, invite, and then encourage participation.

2. From Teammates to Leader

Good team leaders never want yes-men or yes-women. They want direct and honest communication from their people. Even autocratic movie mogul Sam Goldwyn quipped, "I want my people to speak up and be honest, even if it costs them their jobs."

I have always encouraged people on my team to speak openly and directly with me. When we hold meetings, they are often brainstorming sessions where the best idea wins. Often, a team member's remarks or observations really help the team. Sometimes we disagree. That's okay, because we've developed strong enough relationships that we can survive conflict. Getting everything out on the table always improves the team. The one thing I never want to hear from a teammate is, "I could have told you that wouldn't work." If you know it beforehand, that's the time to say it.

Besides directness, the other quality team members need to display when communicating with their leaders is respect. Leading a team isn't easy. It takes hard work. It demands personal sacrifice. It requires making tough and sometimes unpopular decisions. We should respect the person who has agreed to take on that role, and show him or her loyalty.

3. Among Teammates

Charlie Brower remarked, "Few people are successful unless a lot of other people want them to be." For a team to experience success, then all its team members must communicate for the common good. That means exhibiting the following qualities:

- **Being Supportive:** Former NBA player Earvin "Magic" Johnson summed up support by paraphrasing President John F. Kennedy: "Ask not what your teammates can do for you. Ask what you can do for your teammates." When communication is focused on giving rather than getting, it takes the team to a whole new level.

- **Staying Current:** Teammates who rehash old problems and continually open old wounds don't work together. And if they don't work together, they're sunk. As Babe Ruth remarked, "You may have the greatest bunch of individual stars in the world, but if they don't play together, the club won't be worth a dime."

- **Being Vulnerable:** Teams are like little communities, and they develop only when the people in them don't posture with one another. Psychiatrist M. Scott Peck, in his book *The Different Drum*, observes, "If we are to use the word community meaningfully, we must restrict it to a group of individuals who have learned how to communicate honestly with each other, whose relationships go deeper than their masks of composure."

Teams succeed or fail based on the way that team members communicate with one another. As Martin Luther King Jr. said, "We must learn to live together as brothers or perish together as fools." If the interaction is strong, then the action teams take can be strong.

4. Between the Team and the Public

For most teams, communication within the team isn't the only kind that's important. Most teams interact with outsiders in some way, whether those people are clients, customers, or simply the concerned public. When approached by people from outside the group, team members must remember three Rs: They need to be receptive, responsive, and realistic. If they receive communication from others gracefully, always respond in a timely fashion, and are realistic about setting and receiving expectations, they will do well. Outsiders will perceive that their concerns are being received well.

On the other hand, when it comes to communicating to people who are not on the team, the most important quality a team can display is unity. The more independent team members are, the more difficult that can be; it's not easy to get eagles to fly in formation. Yet the power of unity is incredible. One of the principles I always tell my team is that when we are brainstorming and planning, I want all the ideas and criticisms out on the table. We need an opportunity to hash things out. But once we leave the room, we must be united—even if we face opposition or criticism. We remain a strong team.

When it comes down to it, you spell cooperation "we." Working together means winning together. But no team works together unless it's communicating. It takes interaction to fuel action. That's just the way it works.

✑ EVALUATE ✑

Rate your own teamwork abilities by placing the number 1, 2, or 3 next
to each of the following statements:

1 = Never   2 = Sometimes   3 = Always

_____   1. What I say is consistent with what I do.

_____   2. When I give directions or instructions to others there is
rarely confusion or misunderstanding as a result.

_____   3. I enjoy connecting with teammates, and communication
flows freely.

_____   4. I let my leader know about the challenges my team is
facing.

_____   5. When working on a project, I speak up if I see that
something isn't going to work and suggest an alternative.

_____   6. I show my team leader respect and avoid publicly
criticizing him.

_____   7. Once a problem has been faced, talked about, and
resolved, I do not bring it up again.

_____   8. I am receptive to the needs of our clients. I want to know
how we can improve our service.

_____   9. I respond to client concerns quickly and give an honest
and accurate response.

_____   10. I am loyal to my team even in the face of opposition or
criticism.

_____   **Total**

24 – 30   This is an area of strength. Continue growing, but also spend time
helping others to develop in this area.

16 – 23   This area may not be hurting you, but it isn't helping you much
either. To strengthen your teamwork ability, develop yourself in
this area.

10 – 15   This is an area of weakness in your teamwork. Until you grow in
this area, your team effectiveness will be negatively impacted.

❧ DISCUSS ❧

Answer the following questions and discuss your answers when you meet with your team.

1. Why is good communication important to teams?

   _____

   _____

   _____

   _____

   _____

2. How do the leaders of your team communicate with the members of the team? Are the messages consistent, clear, and courteous?

   _____

   _____

   _____

   _____

   _____

3. When you speak with your leader, are you open and direct? Why or why not?

   _____

   _____

   _____

   _____

   _____

4. Is your team united? Explain.

_____

_____

_____

_____

_____

5. How can team members improve communication within the team?

_____

_____

_____

_____

_____

6. How can your team improve its communication with the public?

_____

_____

_____

_____

7. What can you do to get team members to build rapport and open up to one another?

_____

_____

_____

_____

TAKE ACTION

How committed are you to communicating with the other members of your team? Are you supportive of everyone, even the people who aren't your friends? Are you open and vulnerable, even if it's not pleasant? Are you holding a grudge against anyone on the team? If you are, you need to clear the air. If there are *any* barriers to good communication standing between you and another team member, you need to remove them. That is your responsibility.

What are the barriers standing between you and another team member?

_____

_____

_____

_____

Why is it important to improve your attitude toward this person?

_____

_____

_____

_____

What steps will you take to clear the air?

_____

_____

_____

_____

If the other person is not responsive, how will you move on?

_____

_____

_____

_____

15

THE LAW OF
THE EDGE

*The Difference Between Two Equally Talented Teams
Is Leadership*

❧ READ ❧

Teams are always looking for an edge. I'm sure you've seen it: A ball team recruits new talent or develops new plays to beat a tough opponent—or even develops a whole new system to turn around a legacy of losing. Businesses invest in the latest technology, hoping to improve their productivity. Companies fire their ad agencies and hire new ones to launch campaigns, desiring to make gains on big competitors. Corporations cycle through the latest management fads like channel surfers through television reruns. Everyone is seeking the magic formula that will lead to success. The more competitive the field, the more relentless the search.

What is the key to success? Is it talent? Hard work? Technology? Efficiency? To be successful, a team needs all of those things, but it still needs something more. It needs leadership. I believe that . . .

Personnel determine the potential of the team.
Vision determines the direction of the team.
Work ethic determines the preparation of the team.
Leadership determines the success of the team.

Everything rises and falls on leadership. If a team has great leadership, then it can gain everything else it needs to go to the highest level.

Look at any team that has achieved great success, and you will find that it has strong leadership. What enabled General Electric to gain the respect of the corporate world? The leadership edge of Jack Welch. What sealed the victory of the United States in the Persian Gulf War? The leadership edge of Generals Norman Schwarzkopf and Colin Powell. What empowered the Chicago Bulls to win six NBA championships? The leadership edge of Phil Jackson and Michael Jordan. That's why I say the difference between two equally talented teams is leadership. That's the *Law of the Edge.*

If you really want to see the difference that leadership can make, look at the same players on the same team with different leadership. The Los Angeles Lakers are an excellent example. During the late 1990s, they struggled despite having a very talented group of players, including Kobe Bryant, whom many hoped would be the next Michael Jordan, and Shaquille O'Neal, the best center in the game. Both of those players were acquired in 1996, yet they continued to have major problems and never clicked as a team. In 1999, teammate Eddie Jones remarked, "Something isn't right with this team. We're all struggling to keep it together, and with a team that has that much talent, this shouldn't be going on."[1]

The next year, the team brought in Phil Jackson, the man who led the Chicago Bulls to six championships, to coach the Lakers. He kept the same team intact with few changes because he knew talent was not the issue. Of his three key players, O'Neal, Bryant, and Glen Rice, Jackson remarked,

> I think we have three of maybe the most talented players since the time of Kareem and Worthy and Magic. However, Baylor, West and Chamberlain [on the 1968–71 Lakers] outshone even those people. They were three of the greatest scorers in the game, and yet they couldn't win a championship. So yeah, we got the talent, we got the show, we got everything else—but how do you make all the pieces complement each other? That's really what my specialty is as a coach, to try to bring that to bear. And this team is learning that.[2]

Understanding players, bringing them together, and getting them to work together as a team to reach their potential is what leadership is all about. And Jackson provided it. In only one season, the team came together. In 2000 the Lakers won the NBA championship that everyone had believed they had the potential to win. They did it in the same city working under the same conditions and with the same players they'd had in previous years. The only thing that had changed was the leadership. This is what gave them the edge. The difference between two equally talented teams is leadership.

✥ OBSERVE ✥

In essence, leadership is like a running head start for the team. Leaders see farther than their teammates. They see things more quickly than their teammates. They know what's going to happen and can anticipate it. As a result, they get the team moving in the right direction ahead of time, and for that reason the team is in a position to win.

1. Do you agree with the author that every team that has achieved great success has had strong leadership? Explain.

   _____

   _____

   _____

   _____

   _____

2. How does the example of the Lakers' win in 2000 support the *Law of the Edge?*

   _____

   _____

   _____

3. Why isn't talent enough for a team to reach its potential?

   _____

   _____

   _____

4. What team in your industry or area of service models the *Law of the Edge?* How has leadership made the difference?

   _____

   _____

   _____

   _____

   _____

❦ LEARN ❧

With good leadership, everything improves. Leaders are lifters. They push the thinking of their teammates beyond old boundaries of creativity. They elevate others' performance, making them better than they've ever been before. They improve their confidence in themselves and each other. And they raise the expectations of everyone on the team. While managers are often able to maintain a team at its current level, leaders are able to lift it to a higher level than it has ever reached before. The key to this is working with people and bringing out the best in them. For example:

1. **Leaders Transfer Ownership for Work to Those Who Execute the Work.** For a team to succeed, responsibility must go down deep into the organization, down to the roots. This requires a leader who will delegate responsibility and authority to the team. Stephen Covey remarked, "People and organizations don't grow much without delegation and completed staff work, because they are confined to the capacities of the boss and reflect both personal strengths and weaknesses." Good leaders seldom restrict their teams; they release them.

2. **Leaders Create an Environment Where Each Team Member Wants to Be Responsible.** Different people require different kinds of motivation to be their best. One needs encouragement. Another needs to be pushed. Another will rise to a big challenge. Good leaders know how to read people and find the key that will make them take responsibility for their part on the team. But they also remember that they are responsible *to* their people, not *for* them.

3. **Leaders Coach the Development of Personal Capabilities.** The team can reach its potential only if each of the individuals on the team reaches his or her potential. Effective leaders help each player do that. For example, Phil Jackson is well known for giving his players books to read that will help them improve themselves, not just as basketball players but as people.

4. **Leaders Learn Quickly and Encourage Others to Learn Quickly Also.** Leaders lift themselves to a higher level first; then they lift the others around them. Modeling comes first, then leadership. If everyone is improving, then the team is improving.

Leadership is the key to the *Law of the Edge*, but I don't want you to get the idea that the responsibility for leadership always falls on one person. Although most teams have a designated leader who is ultimately responsible for the oversight of the team, the actual leadership of the team is usually shared.

I find that when it comes to leadership, many people tend to see it in one of two ways. The first I call the *Myth of the Head Table*. It's the notion that on a particular team, one person is always in charge in every situation. It's the idea that this particular individual permanently occupies the "head table" in the organization and that everyone else always takes a subordinate role.

The idea that one person is always doing all the leading is false. The same person should not always lead the team in every situation. The challenge of the moment often determines the leader for that challenge, because every person on the team has strengths that come into play. The greater the challenge, the greater the need for the many advantages that leadership provides. And the more leaders a team develops, the greater the edge that leadership provides.

The other misconception about leadership takes the opposite extreme. I call it the *Myth of the Roundtable.* It's the belief that everyone on the team is equal, all opinions count the same, and a team can function without leadership. This isn't true either. A team that tries to function like a democracy never gets anything done.

Everyone is important, but everyone isn't equal. The person with greater experience, skill, and productivity in a given area is more important to the team in that area. General Electric CEO Jack Welch's opinion carries more weight than the person who packs boxes on the assembly line. The NBA's Michael Jordan is worth more money than the guard who sits on the bench. That's the way it is. This doesn't mean that Jack and Michael have more value as *human beings.* In the eyes of God, everyone is loved equally. But when it comes to leading the team, somebody needs to step forward.

The edge that leadership provides is easy to see in sports, but the power of leadership carries over into every field. The business that is run by good leaders often finds its market niche first and outperforms its rivals, even if the rivals possess greater talent. The nonprofit organization headed by strong leaders recruits more people, equips them to lead, and serves a greater number of people as a result. Even in a technical area such as engineering or construction, leadership is invaluable in ensuring the team's success.

❧ EVALUATE ❧

Rate your own teamwork abilities by placing the number 1, 2, or 3 next to each of the following statements:

1 = Never   2 = Sometimes   3 = Always

_____   1. I take complete ownership of my responsibilities.

_____   2. I do my job to the best of my ability so my leader will be able to focus more on the larger challenges our team faces.

_____   3. When my leader suggests a book or resource to me, I usually invest in it.

_____   4. I continually learn from other leaders.

_____   5. I believe that everyone is important, but everyone isn't equal.

_____   6. I treat each member of the team with respect because each person has unique gifts and talents that allow us to be successful.

_____   7. I acknowledge other people's gifts, skills, and abilities, and encourage them to step forward when our team faces a challenge they can help with.

_____   8. I am developing my leadership skills so I will be prepared when called upon.

_____   9. When the team faces a challenge, I think in terms of mobilizing people to meet it.

_____   10. My motivation for taking on a leadership role is to help the team.

_____   **Total**

24 – 30   This is an area of strength. Continue growing, but also spend time helping others to develop in this area.

16 – 23   This area may not be hurting you, but it isn't helping you much either. To strengthen your teamwork ability, develop yourself in this area.

10 – 15   This is an area of weakness in your teamwork. Until you grow in this area, your team effectiveness will be negatively impacted.

✃ DISCUSS ✃

Answer the following questions and discuss your answers when you meet with your team.

1. How are leaders appointed in your organization?

   _____
   _____
   _____
   _____
   _____
   _____

2. What qualities does a person need to lead your team?

   _____
   _____
   _____
   _____
   _____
   _____

3. How can your organization avoid getting caught up in the *Myth of the Head Table* or the *Myth of the Round Table?*

   _____
   _____
   _____
   _____
   _____
   _____

4. What role has leadership played in your team's successes or setbacks?

_____

_____

_____

_____

_____

_____

5. How are you developing your own leadership skills?

_____

_____

_____

_____

_____

_____

6. What changes do you need to make so your leader can do his or her job more effectively?

_____

_____

_____

_____

_____

_____

TAKE ACTION

You don't have to be *the* leader to be *a* leader on your team. Begin the process of improving your leadership skills today. Do the following:

- Acknowledge the value of leadership.
- Take personal responsibility for your own leadership growth.
- Put yourself on a leadership-development program.
- Find a leadership mentor.

Once you have added value to yourself, you will be able to add value to—and influence—others to help your team.

What I am doing to develop better leadership skills:

_____

_____

_____

_____

People who can help me on my leadership journey:

_____

_____

_____

_____

My next step on my leadership journey is to:

_____

_____

_____

_____

16

THE LAW OF HIGH MORALE

When You're Winning, Nothing Hurts

✎ READ ✎

When Rick Hoyt was born in 1962, his parents possessed the typical excited expectations of first-time parents. But then they discovered that during Rick's birth, his umbilical cord had been wrapped around his neck, cutting off the oxygen to his brain. Later, Rick was diagnosed with cerebral palsy. "When he was eight months old," his father, Dick, remembers, "the doctors told us we should put him away—he'd be a vegetable all his life."[1] But Rick's parents wouldn't do that. They were determined to raise him like any other kid.

Sometimes that was tough. Rick is a quadriplegic who cannot speak because he has limited control of his tongue. But Rick's parents worked with him, teaching him everything they could and including him in family activities. When Rick was ten, his life changed when engineers from Tufts University created a device that enabled him to communicate via computer. The first words he slowly and painstakingly punched out were, "Go Bruins." That's when his family, who had been following the NHL's Boston Bruins in the play-offs, found out Rick was a sports fan.

In 1975, after a long battle, the family was finally able to get Rick into public school, where he excelled despite his physical limitations. Rick's world was changing. It changed even more two years later. When Rick found out that a fund-raising 5K race (3.1 miles) was being put on to help a young athlete who had been paralyzed in an accident, he told his father that he wanted to participate.

Dick, a lieutenant colonel in the Air National Guard (who has since retired), was in his late thirties and out of shape. But he agreed to run and push his son in a modified wheelchair. When they crossed the finish line (second to last), Dick recalls, Rick flashed "the biggest smile you ever saw in your life." After the race, Rick wrote out this simple message: "Dad, I felt like I wasn't handicapped." After that day, their lives would never be the same again.

What does a father do when his son, who has never been out of a wheelchair, says that he loves to race? He becomes his boy's hands and feet. That's the day "Team Hoyt" was born. Dick got Rick a more sophisticated racing chair. Then the quadriplegic teenager and the out-of-shape dad began running together—and not casually. Before long, they began training seriously, and in 1981 they ran in their first Boston Marathon together. Since then, they haven't missed a Boston Marathon in twenty years.

After four years of running marathons, the two decided that they were ready for another challenge: triathlons, which combine swimming, cycling, and running. That was no small challenge, especially since Dick would have to learn how to swim! But he did. Dick explained, "He's the one who has motivated me, because if it wasn't for him, I wouldn't be out there competing. What I'm doing is loaning Rick my arms and legs so he can be out there competing like everybody else."[2]

Of all the races in the world, one is considered the toughest—the Ironman Triathlon in Hawaii. The race consists of three back-to-back legs: a 2.4-mile swim, a 112-mile bike race, and a full 26.2-mile marathon run. It's an excruciating test of stamina for any individual. In 1989 Dick and Rick competed in the race together. For the swimming portion, Dick towed a small boat with Rick in it. Then he biked the 112 miles with Rick in a seat on his bicycle handlebars. By the time they got to the running leg, Dick was exhausted.

But it's in these situations that the *Law of High Morale* kicks in. All Dick had to do was remember the words of his son: "When I'm running, my disability seems to disappear. It is the only place where truly I feel as an equal. Due to all the positive feedback, I do not feel handicapped at all. Rather, I feel that I am the intelligent person that I am with no limits."[3]

When you're winning, nothing hurts. By continuing to run, Dick would be winning for his son, and that's what makes all the training and pain worthwhile. Dick loaded Rick into his running chair, and off they went to finish the Ironman. They finished the race in a little over 13 hours and 43 minutes—a very strong time.

Since then, Rick has earned his college degree. He works at Boston University helping to design computer systems for people with disabilities. And, of course, he still competes with his father, who is now over sixty years old. As of March 2001, Team Hoyt had completed a total of 731 races. They've run 53 marathons and 135 triathlons, including four races at Ironman distances. And they will keep running. "There is nothing in the world that the both of us can't conquer together," says Dick.[4] He should know. For almost twenty-five years, he and his teammate have been reaping the rewards of the *Law of High Morale.*

❦ OBSERVE ❧

Dick and Rick Hoyt continually inspire one another and build each other up, to such an extent that their morale is high and they keep winning despite the pain they feel. When a team has high morale, it doesn't just have to deal with whatever circumstances are thrown at it: It creates its own circumstances.

1. What challenges did Dick and Rick Hoyt face?

    _____

    _____

    _____

    _____

2. Why did Rick want to race?

    _____

    _____

    _____

3. How did Dick help his son succeed?

    _____

    _____

    _____

4. Why wouldn't Dick give up when he felt the pain of competition?

    _____

    _____

    _____

    _____

5. What team in your industry or area of service has experienced the *Law of High Morale?* What painful or difficult challenges were they able to overcome because they were winning?

_____

_____

_____

_____

_____

❦ LEARN ❧

The *Law of High Morale* may ring a bell with you, because the phrasing of the law was inspired by the words of Joe Namath, the quarterback who helped the New York Jets win the Super Bowl in 1969. Like any champion, Namath understood that there is an exhilaration that comes from winning. That feeling can be so strong that it sustains you through the discipline, pain, and sacrifice that are required to perform at the highest level.

Perhaps that's why George Allen, who coached the Washington Redskins in the early 1970s, said, "Every time you win, you're reborn; when you lose, you die a little." It's ironic, but if you play hurt, you can put the team in the position to win. And if you win, nothing hurts.

If the team is winning, then morale is high. And if morale is high, then the team is in a position to win. So which comes first: high morale or winning? I believe that high morale usually comes first. Why? Because high morale magnifies everything positive that is happening for a team.

You may be saying, *OK, I agree. When you're winning, nothing hurts. High morale is great for the team. How in the world do we get it?* Let me tell you. If you are a player, then you need to (1) have a good attitude, (2) always give your best, and (3) support the people on the team— players and leaders alike. If you have little influence, then exert what influence you have by modeling excellence.

However, if you're one of the team's leaders, then you have an even greater responsibility. You need to model excellence, but you also need to do more. You need to help the people you lead to develop the kind of morale and momentum that helps create a winning team. The key to knowing what to do can be found in the four stages of morale:

Stage 1: Poor Morale—The Leader Must Do Everything

Nothing is more unpleasant than being on a team when nobody wants to be there. When that is the case, the team is usually negative, lethargic, and without hope. That is often the atmosphere when a team is losing.

If you find yourself in that kind of situation, then do the following:

- *Investigate the situation.* Start by addressing what the team is doing wrong, and begin fixing what's broken. That alone won't give the team high morale, but it will stop giving players reasons to have poor morale.

- *Initiate belief.* The only way for a team to change is if people believe in themselves. As the leader, you must initiate that belief. Show people you believe in yourself and in them.

- *Create energy.* The desire to change without the energy to change just frustrates people. To bring a greater level of energy to the team, you need to be energetic. Work with energy long enough, and someone on the team will eventually come alongside you and join you. Then another person will. Eventually, the energy will spread.

- *Communicate hope.* The greatest need of players at this stage is hope. As Napoleon Bonaparte said, "Leaders are dealers in hope." Help them to see the potential of the team.

In stage one, the only way to get the ball rolling is to start pushing it yourself. As the leader, you can't wait for someone else to do it.

Stage 2: Low Morale—The Leader Must Do Productive Things

In the beginning, any movement is a great victory. But to create positive morale, you need to pick up some speed. You need to be productive. After all, you can't steer a parked car! To get the team moving:

- *Model behavior that has a high return.* People do what people see. The best way for them to learn what you expect of them is to model it yourself.

- *Develop relationships with people of potential.* To get any team going in the right direction, you need players who can produce. At this stage, your team may have some producers. If so, develop relationships with them. If it doesn't, then find the people who have the potential to be productive, and start with them. Don't ask too much of them too soon. Leaders touch a heart before they ask for a hand. That's why you want to begin by building relationships.

- *Set up small victories and talk teammates through them.* Nothing helps people grow in skill and confidence like having some wins under their belts. That's what you want to give the people on your team. Begin with the people who have the greatest potential.

- *Communicate vision.* As I explain in the *Law of the Compass,* vision gives team members direction and confidence. Keep the vision before your team continually.

Once you've got the team really moving, then you can begin to steer.

Stage 3: Moderate Morale—The Leader Must Do Difficult Things

Getting the team together and moving is an accomplishment. But where you're going matters. To change from simply *moving the team* to *moving the team in the right direction,* you've got to begin doing the difficult things that help the team to improve and develop high morale:

- *Make changes that make the team better.* Leaders are responsible for minimizing the damage any team member can do because of weakness or attitude, and for maximizing the effectiveness of all team members by placing them in their proper niche. Often those actions require tough decisions.

- *Receive the buy-in of team members.* It's one thing to cast vision to the team. It's another to get your teammates to buy in. Yet to build higher morale, that is what you must do. The team must buy into you as a leader, embrace the values and mission of the team, and align themselves with your expectations. If you can do that, you will be able to take the team where it needs to go.

- *Communicate commitment.* Part of the process of getting people to buy in comes from showing them your commitment. The *Law of Buy-In* from *The 21 Irrefutable Laws of Leadership* says that people buy into the leader, then into the vision. If you have consistently demonstrated high competence, good character, and strong commitment, you have laid the foundation for your people to buy in.

- *Develop and equip members for success.* Nothing builds morale like success. Most people are not capable of achieving success on their own. They need help, and that is one of the primary reasons for anyone to lead them. If you invest in your team-mates, then you help them and the team succeed.

The two toughest stages in the life of the team are the first stage, where you are trying to create movement in a team that's going nowhere, and the third stage, where you must become a change agent. Those are the times when leadership is most needed. And stage 3 is the make-or-break time for a leader. If you can succeed in stage 3, then you will be able to create high morale in your team.

Stage 4: High Morale—The Leader Must Do Little Things

In stage four, your job as a leader is to help the team maintain high morale and momentum:

- *Keep the team focused and on course.* High morale leads to winning, and winning maintains morale. That's why it's important to keep team members focused. If they lose focus or get off course, then they'll stop winning. And remember, the farther you intend to go, the greater the impact of an error in direction. If you want to cross a street, being a degree or two off course doesn't hurt you. If you want to cross the ocean, a few degrees can get you into a lot of trouble.

- *Communicate successes.* One of the things that helps people stay on track is to know what they're doing right. You can indicate this by communicating the team's successes. There's nothing that boosts morale like winning and then celebrating it.

- *Remove morale mashers.* Once the team is rolling in the right direction, keep it rolling. The *Law of the Big Mo* from *The 21 Irrefutable Laws of Leadership* says that momentum is a leader's best friend. Leaders see before others do, so they need to protect the team from the things that will hurt the team.

- *Allow other leaders to lead.* When a leader prepares other team members to lead and then turns them loose to do it, it does two things. First, it uses the momentum the team already has to create new leaders for the team. It's easier to make new leaders successful if they are part of a successful team. Second, it increases the leadership of the team. And that makes the team even more successful. If a leader continually does that, he or she can create a cycle of success that feeds the team's high morale.

You don't have to have the power of a president or the ability of an Olympic athlete to practice the *Law of High Morale.* You can apply the principle to your business, volunteer service, or even your family. The process of building high morale is simple, but it isn't easy. It takes strong leadership, and it takes time.

❧ EVALUATE ❧

Rate your own teamwork abilities by placing the number 1, 2, or 3 next to each of the following statements:

1 = Never   2 = Sometimes   3 = Always

_____	1. I give my best to the team.
_____	2. I support my fellow team members.
_____	3. I support team leaders.
_____	4. I maintain a positive attitude despite circumstances.
_____	5. I believe in myself and my abilities.
_____	6. I believe in the abilities of my teammates and encourage them.
_____	7. I maximize my leadership role based on the morale of the team.
_____	8. I have developed healthy working relationships with the people on my team.
_____	9. I help to keep momentum going for the team.
_____	10. I celebrate my achievements and the achievements of my team.

_____   **Total**

24 – 30 This is an area of strength. Continue growing, but also spend time helping others to develop in this area.

16 – 23 This area may not be hurting you, but it isn't helping you much either. To strengthen your teamwork ability, develop yourself in this area.

10 – 15 This is an area of weakness in your teamwork. Until you grow in this area, your team effectiveness will be negatively impacted.

❦ DISCUSS ❧

Answer the following questions and discuss your answers when you meet with your team.

1. Do you agree that "when you're winning, nothing hurts"? Explain.

    _____

    _____

    _____

    _____

    _____

    _____

2. Why is it important for your team to have high morale?

    _____

    _____

    _____

    _____

    _____

    _____

3. Which stage of morale is your team in? Why?

    _____

    _____

    _____

    _____

    _____

    _____

4. What are some ways your team can improve its morale?

_____

_____

_____

_____

_____

_____

5. What should the team's leaders be doing to improve morale?

_____

_____

_____

_____

_____

_____

6. What are you willing to do personally to get your team to win or keep winning?

_____

_____

_____

_____

_____

_____

TAKE ACTION

If you want to reap the rewards of the *Law of High Morale*, you can't wait until your morale is high to begin performing. You need to act your way into feeling, not feel your way into acting. Begin by performing at a level of excellence appropriate for someone who's experiencing a winning season. Your dedication and enthusiasm will help your performance—and it will begin to inspire some of your teammates.

List the actions you will take to heighten your morale in these three areas:

Attitude:

_____
_____
_____
_____
_____

Performance:

_____
_____
_____
_____
_____

Communication with others:

_____
_____
_____
_____
_____

THE LAW OF
DIVIDENDS

Investing in the Team Compounds over Time

❧ READ ❧

He's one of the greatest team builders in all of sports, yet you've probably never heard of him. Take a look at these impressive accomplishments:

- 40 consecutive basketball seasons with at least 20 wins

- 5 national championships

- #1 ranking in his region in 20 of the last 33 years

- Lifetime winning percentage of .870

His name is Morgan Wootten. And why have most people never heard of him? Because he is a *high school* basketball coach!

When asked to name the greatest basketball coach of all time, most people would respond with one of two names: Red Auerbach or John Wooden. But here is what John Wooden, the UCLA coach called the "Wizard of Westwood," has to say about Morgan Wootten:

People say Morgan Wootten is the best high school coach in the country. I disagree. I know of no finer coach at any level—high school, college, or pro. I've said it elsewhere and I'll say it here: I stand in awe of him.[1]

That's a pretty strong recommendation from the man who won ten NCAA national championships and coached some of the most talented players in the game, including Kareem Abdul-Jabbar. (By the way, when Jabbar was in high school at Power Memorial Academy, his team lost only one game—to Morgan Wootten's team!)

Morgan Wootten never planned to coach a team. He was a decent athlete in high school, but nothing special. However, he was an excellent talker. Growing up, his ambition was to be an attorney. But when he was a nineteen-year-old college student, a friend tricked him into accepting a job coaching kids from an orphanage in baseball, a game he knew little about. The team had no uniforms and no equipment. And despite working hard, they lost all sixteen of their games.

During that first season, Wootten fell in love with those kids. When they asked him to come back and coach football, he couldn't refuse them. Besides, he had played football in high school, so he knew something about it. The orphanage team went undefeated and won the Washington, D.C., CYO championship. But more important, Wootten began to realize that he wanted to invest his time in children, not in court cases.

Even that first year he began making a difference in the lives of kids. He remembers one boy in particular who had started stealing and was repeatedly brought back to the orphanage by the police. He described the boy as having "two-and-a-half strikes against him already." Wootten let the boy know he was headed for trouble. But he also took the boy under his wing. Wootten recalled,

We started spending some time together. I took him to my house, and he'd enjoy Mom's meals. He spent weekends with us. He became friends with my brother and sisters. He's still in Washington today and doing quite well and known to a lot of people. Anyone would be proud to call him their son. He was bound for a life of crime and jail, however, and maybe a lot worse, until someone gave him the greatest gift a parent can give a child—his time.[2]

Giving of himself to the people on his teams is something Wootten has done every year since then. Virginia Military Institute coach Marty Fletcher, a former player and assistant under Wootten, summarized his talent this way: "His secret is that he makes whomever he is with feel like the most important person in the world."[3]

It wasn't long before Wootten was invited to become an assistant coach at a local powerhouse high school. Then with a couple of years' experience under his belt, he became head coach at DeMatha High School.

When he got started at the school in 1956, Wootten was taking over a bunch of losing teams. He called together all the students who wanted to play sports at DeMatha, and this is what he told them:

Fellas, things are going to change. I know how bad DeMatha's teams have been during these last few years, but that's over with. We're going to win at DeMatha and we're going to build a *tradition* of winning. Starting right now . . . But let me tell you how we're going to do it. We're going to outwork every team we ever play . . . With a lot of hard work and discipline and dedication, people are going to hear about us and respect us, because DeMatha will be a winner.[4]

That year the football team won half its games, which was quite an accomplishment. In basketball and baseball, they were division champions. His teams have been winning ever since. DeMatha has long been considered a dynasty.

On October 13, 2000, Wootten was inducted into the Naismith Basketball Hall of Fame in Springfield, Massachusetts. At that time, his teams had amassed a record of 1,210-183. Over the years, more than 250 of his players have won college scholarships. Twelve players from his high school teams have gone on to play in the NBA.[5]

But winning games and honors isn't what excites Wootten most. It's investing in the kids. Wootten says,

> Coaches at every level have a tendency to lose sight of their purpose at times, especially after success arrives. They start to put the cart before the horse by working harder and harder to develop their teams, using their boys or girls to do it, gradually forgetting that their real purpose should be to develop the kids, using their teams to do it.[6]

Wootten's attitude reaps rewards not only for a team, but for the individuals on the team. For example, for a twenty-six-year stretch, every single one of Wootten's seniors earned college scholarships—not just starters, but bench players too. Penn State assistant coach Chuck Swenson observed, "Even if you know a kid isn't a great player, if he's a DeMatha player, he'll help your program. With Morgan, you know you're getting a quality kid, who will make good grades and work hard for you."[7] Gary Williams, head coach of the University of Maryland, says, "His players are so fundamentally sound, do so many things right, that they may not improve as much as kids in another program who haven't been as well coached . . . These aren't raw talents: They're refined ones."[8] What's remarkable is that this is being said of *high school* students, not college players or pros.

❦ OBSERVE ❧

Investing in the team compounds over time. Morgan Wootten invests in his players because it is the right thing to do, because he cares about them. This practice has made his players good, his teams successful, and his career remarkable. He is the first basketball coach to have won 1,200 games at any level. Developing people pays off in every way.

1. In what ways has Morgan Wootten invested in his players?

2. How have people invested in you?

3. Why did people take time to invest in you?

4. How has investing in another person made your job easier?

_____

_____

_____

_____

5. What team in your industry or area of service practices the
   Law of Dividends? How has their investment in their team
   members compounded over time?

_____

_____

_____

_____

⚜ LEARN ⚜

Throughout this workbook you've read about people who have dedicated themselves to investing in the people on their teams. And those investments pay all kinds of rich dividends. Gordon Bethune's investment of trust has paid off by keeping Continental Airlines in business and saving the jobs of its fourteen thousand employees. The investment of Bernie Marcus and Arthur Blank is paying dividends to the employees who own Home Depot stock, including one thousand employee-millionaires. And Lilly Tartikoff's investment in people is paying dividends in cancer research.

Usually the time, money, and effort it takes to develop team members don't change the team overnight, but they always pay off. Investing in the team compounds over time.

I believe that most people recognize that investing in a team brings benefits to everyone on the team. The question for most people isn't why, but how. Allow me to share with you ten steps you can take to invest in your team. You can implement these practices whether you are a player or coach, employee or employer, follower or leader. There is always someone on the team who can benefit from what you have to offer. And when everyone on the team is investing, then the benefits are like those of compound interest: They multiply.

Start investing in your team by

1. Making the Decision to Build a Team—This Starts the Investment in the Team

It's said that every journey begins with the first step. Deciding that people on the team are worth developing is the first step in building a better team. This requires *commitment.*

2. Gathering the Best Team Possible—This Elevates the Potential of the Team

As I've previously remarked, the better the people on the team, the greater the potential. There's only one kind of team that you may be a part of where you *shouldn't* go out and find the best players available, and that's family. You need to stick with those teammates through thick and thin. But every other kind of team can benefit from the recruitment of the very best people available.

3. Paying the Price to Develop the Team—This Ensures the Growth of the Team

When Morgan Wootten extended himself to benefit the kid who had two and a half strikes against him, he and his family had to pay a price to help that boy. It wasn't convenient or comfortable. It cost them energy, money, and time.

It will cost you to develop your team. You will have to dedicate time that could be used for personal productivity. You will have to spend money that could be used for personal benefit. And sometimes you will have to set aside your personal agenda. But the benefit to the individuals—and the team—is worth the price. Everything you give is an investment.

4. Doing Things Together as a Team—This Provides Community for the Team

I once read the statement: "Even when you've played the game of your life, it's the feeling of teamwork that you'll remember. You'll forget the plays, the shots, and the scores, but you'll never forget your teammates."[9] This remark describes the community that develops among teammates who spend time doing things together.

The only way to develop community and cohesiveness among your teammates is to get them together, not just in a professional setting but in personal ones as well. There are lots of good ways to connect with your teammates, and to connect them with one another. Many families who want to bond together find that camping does the trick. Business colleagues can socialize outside of work (in an appropriate way). The where and when are not as important as the fact that team members share common experiences.

5. Empowering Team Members with Responsibility and Authority— This Raises Up Leaders for the Team

The greatest growth for people often occurs as a result of the trial and error of personal experience. Any team that wants people to step up to a higher level of performance—and to higher levels of leadership—must give team members authority as well as responsibility. If you are a leader on your team, don't protect your position or hoard your power. Give it away. That's the only way to empower your team.

6. Giving Credit for Success to the Team—This Lifts the Morale of the Team

Mark Twain said, "I can live for two months on one good compliment." That's the way most people feel. They are willing to work hard if they receive recognition for their efforts. That's why Napoleon Bonaparte observed, "A soldier will fight long and hard for a bit of colored ribbon." Compliment your teammates. Talk up their accomplishments. And if you are the leader, take the blame but never the credit. Do this, and your team will always fight for you.

7. Watching to See That the Investment in the Team Is Paying Off—This Brings Accountability to the Team

If you put money into an investment play, you expect a return—maybe not right away, but certainly over time. How will you know whether you are gaining or losing ground on that investment? You have to pay attention to it and measure its progress.

The same is true of an investment in people. You need to observe whether you are getting a return for the time, energy, and resources you are putting into them. Some people develop quickly. Others are slower to respond, and that's OK. The main thing you want to see is progress.

8. Stopping Your Investment in Players Who Do Not Grow—This Eliminates Greater Losses for the Team

One of the most difficult experiences for any team member is leaving a teammate behind. Yet that is what you must do if someone on your team refuses to grow or change for the benefit of his or her teammates. As I mentioned in the *Law of the Chain*, this doesn't mean that you value the person less. It just means you stop spending your time trying to invest in someone who won't or can't make the team better.

9. Creating New Opportunities for the Team—This Allows the Team to Stretch

There is no greater investment you can make in a team than giving it new opportunities. When a team has the possibility of taking new ground or facing new challenges, it has to stretch. This process not only gives the team a chance to grow, but it also benefits every individual. Everyone has the opportunity to grow toward his or her potential.

10. Giving the Team the Best Possible Chance to Succeed—This Guarantees the Team a High Return

James E. Hunton says, "Coming together is a beginning. Keeping together is progress. Working together is success." One of the most important things you can do is clear away obstacles so that your team has the best possible chance to work together for success. If you are a team member, this may mean personal sacrifice or helping others to work together better. If you are a leader, this means creating a great environment for the team and giving each person what he or she needs at any given time to ensure success.

One of the great things about investing in a team is that it almost guarantees a high return for the effort, because a team can do so much more than individuals working alone. Or, as Rex Murphy, one of my conference attendees, told me: "Where there's a will, there's a way; where there's a team, there's more than one way."

❧ EVALUATE ❧

Rate your own teamwork abilities by placing the number 1, 2, or 3 next to each of the following statements:

1 = Never   2 = Sometimes   3 = Always

_____ 1. I believe that the people on my team are worth investing in.

_____ 2. I make sacrifices to develop others.

_____ 3. I share common experiences with my teammates by including them in activities.

_____ 4. I am tolerant of a person's trials and errors when he or she is doing new things, learning, and trying to improve.

_____ 5. I give credit to the members of my team.

_____ 6. I am willing to give away some of my power to other members on the team.

_____ 7. I pay attention to the progress of my teammates.

_____ 8. If someone is not willing to learn or change, I will accept this and find someone else to invest in.

_____ 9. I am investing in at least one person on my team.

_____ 10. I believe that my teammates' improvement will bring the team success.

_____ **Total**

24 – 30   This is an area of strength. Continue growing, but also spend time helping others to develop in this area.

16 – 23   This area may not be hurting you, but it isn't helping you much either. To strengthen your teamwork ability, develop yourself in this area.

10 – 15   This is an area of weakness in your teamwork. Until you grow in this area, your team effectiveness will be negatively impacted.

❧ DISCUSS ❧

Answer the following questions and discuss your answers when you meet with your team.

1. List two or three unique skills and talents for each person on your team.

   _____

   _____

   _____

   _____

   _____

   _____

2. Are you an investor or an investee on the team? Explain.

   _____

   _____

   _____

   _____

   _____

   _____

3. How have you invested in another member of your team?

   _____

   _____

   _____

   _____

   _____

   _____

4. How has your team developed community and cohesiveness?

_____

_____

_____

_____

_____

5. How does your team celebrate success?

_____

_____

_____

_____

_____

6. Give an example of how you have been empowered and given responsibility. What was the result?

_____

_____

_____

_____

_____

7. What will you do in the coming weeks and months to invest in your team?

_____

_____

_____

_____

_____

TAKE ACTION

Are you giving a good return on what your teammates are investing in you? Think about the opportunities you have received and the positive learning experiences to which you've been exposed. Have you seized all of them enthusiastically, or have you allowed many of them to slip by?

If you've been too lackadaisical about pursuing growth opportunities, then change your attitude today. Grow all you can, and determine to give the team a good return on its investment in you.

Areas that I need to grow in:

_____
_____
_____

People on my team who can help me improve my skills:

_____
_____
_____

Outside sources that can help me improve my skills:

_____
_____
_____

People I will invest in:

_____
_____
_____

How I will invest in them:

_____
_____
_____

NOTES

CHAPTER 1

1. Brandon Tartikoff and Charles Leerhsen, *The Last Great Ride* (New York: Turtle Bay Books, 1992), 60.
2. "OncoLink: An Interview with Lilly Tartikoff," <www.oncolink.upenn.edu>.

CHAPTER 2

1. Frye Gaillard, *If I Were a Carpenter: Twenty Years of Habitat for Humanity* (Winston-Salem, NC: John F. Blair, 1995).
2. "The History of Habitat," <www.habitat.org>.

CHAPTER 3

1. "Bush Nominates Powell as Secretary of State," <www.usatoday.com> December 17, 2000.
2. Colin Powell with Joseph E. Persico, *My American Journey* (New York: Random House, 1995), 28.
3. Michael Hirsh and John Barry, "Leader of the Pack," *Newsweek*, December 25, 2000.
4. "Town Hall Meeting: January 25, 2001," <www.state.gov>.

CHAPTER 4

1. "Mount Everest History/Facts," <www.mnteverest.com>.
2. Ulman, *Man of Everest:* The Autobiography of Tenzing (London, George & Harrap Co., 1955) 250.
3. Ibid., 255.
4. Ibid., 227.

CHAPTER 5

1. "Quick Answers to the Most Frequently Asked Questions," <www.oilspill.state.ak.us/history/history>.
2. "Exxon's Appeal of the Valdez Oil Spill $5 Billion in Punitive Judgment," <www.exxon.mobil.com>.
3. Danny Cox with John Hoover, *Leadership When the Heat's On* (New York: McGraw-Hill, 1992), 69–70.

CHAPTER 6

1. "The President Suits up for Practice," <www.cbs.sportsline.com>.

CHAPTER 7

1. Greg Farrell, "Building a New Big Blue," November 23, 1999, <www.usatoday.com>.
2. "IBM Wants Business Partners to Focus on Growth," March 2, 1999, <www.findarticles.com>.
3. Farrell, "Building a New Big Blue."
4. Michelle Marchetti, "IBM's Marketing Visionary," *Sales and Marketing Management,* September 2000, 55.
5. Proverbs 29:18 KJV.

CHAPTER 8

1. John C. Maxwell, *The Winning Attitude* (Nashville: Thomas Nelson, 1993), 24.

CHAPTER 9

1. "Interview with Stacey Loizeaux," <www.pbs.org/wgbh/nova/kaboom>.
2. John C. Maxwell, *The 21 Irrefutable Laws of Leadership: Follow Them and People Will Follow You* (Nashville: Thomas Nelson, 1998), 58.
3. Barry J. Gibbons, *This Indecision Is Final: 32 Management Secrets of Albert Einstein, Billie Holiday, and a Bunch of Other People Who Never Worked 9 to 5* (Chicago: Irwin Professional Publishing, 1996).
4. Colossians 3:23–24.
5. John Carl Roat, *Class-29: The Making of U.S. Navy SEALs* (New York: Ballantine Books, 1998), 135–36.

CHAPTER 10

1. Stephen Franklin, "Founder a Force in Retail, Civic Affairs," <www.chicagotribune.com>, December 29, 2000.
2. "End of the Line," <www.nytimes.com>, December 29, 2000.
3. "Historical Chronology—1925: Opening Retail Stores," <www.sears.com>, March 15, 2001.
4. Allan Cox, *Straight Talk for Monday Morning* (New York: John Wiley & Sons).
5. John C. Maxwell, *The 21 Indispensable Qualities of a Leader: Becoming the Person Others Will Want to Follow* (Nashville: Thomas Nelson, 1999), 144–45.

CHAPTER 11

1. Michael D. Eisner with Tony Schwartz, *Work in Progress* (New York: Random House, 1998), 171.
2. John Taylor, *Storming the Magic Kingdom: Wall Street Raiders and the Battle for Disney* (New York: Alfred A. Knopf, 1987), 14.
3. Eisner, *Work in Progress,* 235.
4. "The Walt Disney Company Annual Report 2000: Financial Review," <www.disney.go.com>, March 28, 2001.

CHAPTER 13

1. Bernie Marcus and Arthur Blank with Bob Andelman, *Built from Scratch: How a Couple of Regular Guys Grew the Home Depot from Nothing to $30 Billion* (New York: Times Business, 1999), xvi–xvii.
2. "Company Information," <www.homedepot.com>, April 11, 2001.
3. Marcus and Blank, *Built from Scratch*, xvii.

CHAPTER 14

1. Gordon Bethune with Scott Huler, *From Worst to First: Behind the Scenes of Continental's Remarkable Comeback* (New York: John Wiley and Sons, 1998), 4.
2. Bethune, *From Worst to First*, 6.
3. Thomas A. Stewart, "Just Think: No Permission Needed," *Fortune*, January 8, 2001, <www.fortune.com>.
4. Bethune, *From Worst to First*, 211.

CHAPTER 15

1. Mike Kahn, "Harris's Del-etion No Surprise," <www.cbs.sportsline.com>, February 24, 1999.
2. Mike Rowland, *Los Angeles Magazine*, June 2000, <www.findarticles.com>.

CHAPTER 16

1. David Tereshchuk, "Racing Towards Inclusion," <www.teamhoyt.com>, March 14, 2001.
2. "Father-Son Duo Are World Class Competitors, Despite Odds," <www.cnn.com>, November 29, 1999.
3. Ibid.
4. Ibid.

CHAPTER 17

1. Don Banks, "Teacher First, Seldom Second, Wootten Has Built Monument to Excellence at Maryland's DeMatha High," *St. Petersburg Times*, April 3, 1987, <www.dematha.org>.
2. Ibid.
3. John Feinstein, "A Down-to-Earth Coach Brings DeMatha to New Heights," *Washington Post*, February 27, 1984, <www.dematha.org>.
4. Morgan Wootten and Bill Gilbert, *From Orphans to Champions: The Story of DeMatha's Morgan Wootten* (New York: Atheneum, 1979), 24–25.
5. William Plummer, "Wooten's Way," *People*, November 20, 2000, 166.
6. Wooten and Gilbert, *From Orphans to Champions*, 12–13.
7. Feinstein, "A Down-to-Earth Coach Brings DeMatha to New Heights."
8. Ibid.
9. Source unknown.

ABOUT THE AUTHOR

JOHN C. MAXWELL, known as America's expert on leadership, is founder of The INJOY Group™, an organization dedicated to helping people maximize their personal and leadership potential. Each year Maxwell speaks in person to more than 350,000 people and influences the lives of more than one million people through seminars, books, and tapes. He is the bestselling author of more than twenty-five books, including *The 21 Irrefutable Laws of Leadership, Failing Forward, Developing the Leader Within You,* and *The 21 Indispensable Qualities of a Leader.*

How Can You Be A More Successful Team Leader?

John C. Maxwell has the resources for you!

STEP 1 | ## Assess Your Team Leadership Skills

Take the FREE online assessment at **www.LawsOfTeamwork.com/Workbook**. You will immediately see a snapshot of your leadership ability and how well you create and lead teams.

STEP 2 | ## Start With The Basics

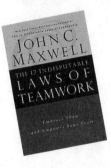

Spend 17 days reading *The 17 Indisputable Laws of Teamwork*. Read one chapter each day to understand the foundations for building and leading solid teams.

Leadership expert John C. Maxwell encourages readers to explore and enhance their teamwork skills. John examines how a group of individuals can come together and succeed by outlining principles for building, enhancing, and working as a team.

These principles can be used in any business, family or organization. No matter who you are, if you learn and apply the laws, your teamwork capacity will increase and your efforts will be multiplied.

STEP 3   Invest In Yourself And Your Team

Audio Series

Living the 17 Essential Qualities of a Team Player: Becoming the Kind of Person Every Team Wants
— Audio Application Series

Invest 17 weeks in a personal growth plan that will make you the kind of player every team wants. *Living the 17 Essential Qualities of a Team Player* is an in-depth course, which will supply you with the information and application you need to become more valuable and effective in any team setting.

Video Series

Learning the 17 Indisputable Laws of Teamwork
— Video Application Series

Spend 17 weeks investing in your people by taking them through the *Learning the 17 Indisputable Laws of Teamwork* series. As a team, set aside one hour each week to study one session. The course is designed to teach each person — leaders and followers — how to form productive teams and participate as effective team members.

You will learn:
- The benefits of teamwork
- To identify the role and importance of each team member
- How to motivate and enhance the team
- What makes a team successful and how to maintain the team's success

STEP 4   Continue The Process

Let John C. Maxwell mentor you monthly.

Maximum Impact® The Monthly Mentoring Leadership Club for Marketplace Leaders
— Audio Program (Available on CD or audiocassette)

Most leaders will agree that regardless of how long they've been in a leadership position, there are issues that they face every day where they would like some insight and helpful perspective. John will provide you with such mentorship on a monthly basis.

For More Information or to Order...
Visit www.LawsOfTeamwork.com/Workbook

The INJOY Group™
A Lifelong Partner Dedicated to Lifting Your Potential

The INJOY Group™, founded in 1985 by Dr. John C. Maxwell, dedicates itself to adding value to individuals and organizations across America and around the world. It accomplishes its mission by forging lasting partnerships that foster personal growth and organizational effectiveness.

The INJOY Group™ consists of . . .

INJOY® Resources—Equipping People to Succeed

INJOY® Conferences—Empowering Leaders to Excel

INJOY® Stewardship Services—Energizing Churches to Raise
      Funds for Financing the Future

EQUIP™—Affecting Leadership Development in Emerging
    Countries, American Urban Centers, and Academic
    Communities

Each year, The INJOY Group™ partners with tens of thousands of people, dozens of church denominations, and countless business and nonprofit organizations to help people reach their potential.

To contact Dr. John C. Maxwell or any division of The INJOY Group™, call, write, or E-mail us:

The INJOY Group
P.O. Box 7700
Atlanta, GA 30357-0700
800-333-6506
www.INJOY.com

Books by Dr. John C. Maxwell
Can Teach You How to Be a REAL Success

RELATIONSHIPS
Becoming a Person of Influence (Thomas Nelson)
The Power of Partnership in the Church (J. Countryman)
The Treasure of a Friend (J. Countryman)

EQUIPPING
Developing the Leaders Around You (Thomas Nelson)
Partners in Prayer (Thomas Nelson)
The 17 Indisputable Laws of Teamwork (Thomas Nelson)
The 17 Essential Qualities of a Team Player (Thomas Nelson)
Success One Day at a Time (J. Countryman)
Your Road Map for Success (Thomas Nelson)
Your Road Map for Success Workbook (Thomas Nelson)

ATTITUDE
Attitude 101 (Thomas Nelson, 2003)
Failing Forward (Thomas Nelson)
Living at the Next Level (Thomas Nelson)
The Winning Attitude (Thomas Nelson)
Your Bridge to a Better Future (Thomas Nelson)

LEADERSHIP
Developing the Leader Within You (Thomas Nelson)
Developing the Leader Within You Workbook (Thomas Nelson)
Leadership 101 (Thomas Nelson)
Leadership Promises for Every Day (J. Countryman, 2003)
Leading from the Lockers (Tommy Nelson, children's book)
The Maxwell Leadership Bible (Thomas Nelson Bible)
The 21 Indispensable Qualities of a Leader (Thomas Nelson)
The 21 Irrefutable Laws of Leadership (Thomas Nelson)
The 21 Irrefutable Laws of Leadership Workbook (Thomas Nelson)
The Right to Lead (J. Countryman)

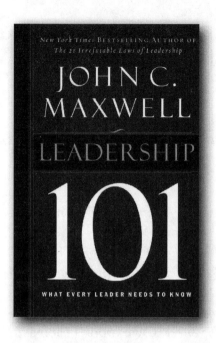

Drawing from John Maxwell's bestsellers *Developing the Leader Within You, The 21 Irrefutable Laws of Leadership, The 21 Indispensable Qualities of a Leader,* and *Becoming a Person of Influence, Leadership 101* explores the timeless principles that have become Dr. Maxwell's trademark style. In a concise, straightforward style, Maxwell focuses on essential and time-tested qualities necessary for true leadership—influence, integrity, attitude, vision, problem-solving, and self-discipline— and guides readers through practical steps to develop true leadership in their lives and the lives of others.

ISBN: 0-7852-6419-1

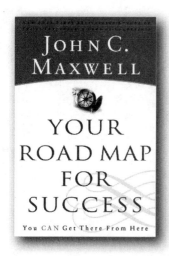

Defining success is a difficult task. Most people equate it with wealth, power, and happiness. However, true success is not a thing you acquire or achieve. Rather, it is a journey you take your whole life long.

In a refreshingly straightforward style, John Maxwell shares unique insights into what it means to be successful. And he reveals a definition that puts genuine success within your reach yet motivates you to keep striving for your dreams.

I want to help you discover your personal road map for success, teach you what it means to be on the success journey, answer many of your questions, and equip you with what you'll need to change yourself and keep growing.

—JOHN C. MAXWELL

ISBN: 0-7852-6596-1

What is the definition of success? Some people believe it is defined through money and power. John C. Maxwell teaches that success is not something that can be acquired. Rather, it is a journey. Maxwell reveals that success is not limited to those with big bank accounts or special abilities. Success can be achieved by anyone willing to apply a few practical principles to their daily lives.

An excellent enhancement for the book by the same name, this workbook teaches readers the keys to success and how to apply them to their everyday lives.

ISBN: 0-7852-6575-9